LONDON RECORD SOCIETY
PUBLICATIONS

VOLUME XIII
FOR THE YEAR 1977

THE CHURCH IN LONDON
1375–1392

A. K. McHARDY

LONDON RECORD SOCIETY
1977

© *London Record Society*
SBN 9009 5213 X

THIS VOLUME IS PUBLISHED WITH THE HELP
OF A GRANT FROM THE LATE
MISS ISOBEL THORNLEY'S BEQUEST TO
THE UNIVERSITY OF LONDON

Printed in Great Britain by
W & J MACKAY LIMITED, CHATHAM, KENT

CONTENTS

ABBREVIATIONS

Bodl. Libr. MS Film 651	Register of Henry Despenser bishop of Norwich (on microfilm)
Butler, 'Braybrooke'	L. H. Butler, 'Robert Braybrooke Bishop of London (1381–1404) and his Kinsmen', unpublished Oxford D.Phil. thesis (1951)
C 85	P.R.O. Chancery, Significations of excommunication
C.C.R.	*Calendar of Close Rolls*
C.F.R.	*Calendar of Fine Rolls*
C.P.R.	*Calendar of Patent Rolls*
E 135	P.R.O. Exchequer, King's Remembrancer, Ecclesiastical documents
E 179	P.R.O. Exchequer, Clerical subsidies
E 202	P.R.O. Exchequer, Returned writs
Emden, *Cambridge*	A. B. Emden, *A Biographical Register of the University of Cambridge to 1500* (1963)
Emden, *Oxford*	A. B. Emden, *A Biographical Register of the University of Oxford to A.D. 1500*, 3 vols. (1957–9)
John Lydford's Book	*John Lydford's Book*, ed. D. M. Owen (Historical Manuscripts Commission JP 22, 1974)
L.A.O.	Lincolnshire Archives Office. Use has been made of Registers 10 (John Buckingham, Institutions 1), 12 (John Buckingham, Memoranda), 12B (John Buckingham, Royal Writs)
L.R.2	P.R.O. Exchequer, Miscellaneous books
mr	magister
Reg. Arundel (Ely)	Cambridge University Library, Ely Diocesan Registers, Register of Thomas Arundel
Reg. Brantingham	Devon County Record Office, Register of Thomas Brantingham
Reg. Courtenay (Heref.)	Hereford Diocesan Registry, Register of William Courtenay
Reg. Sudbury (Cant.)	Lambeth Palace Library, Register of Simon Sudbury
Reg. Sudbury (London)	*Registrum Simonis de Sudbiria*, ed. R. C. Fowler, 2 vols. (Canterbury and York Society, vols. xxxiv, xxxviii, 1927, 1938)
Reg. Wakefeld	*Register of Henry Wakefeld*, ed. W. P. Marett (Worcs. Historical Society, N.S.vii, 1972)
Reg. Wykeham	Hampshire Record Office, Register of William of Wykeham

Reign of Richard II	*The Reign of Richard II*, ed. F. R. H. Du Boulay and C. M. Barron (1971)
Rot. Parl.	*Rotuli Parliamentorum*, ed. J. Strachey *et al.*, 6 vols. (Record Commission, 1767–77)
Taxatio	*Taxatio Ecclesiastica Angliae et Walliae auctoritate P. Nicholai IV circa A.D. 1291* (Record Commission, 1802)
V.C.H.	*Victoria County History*
W.A.M.	Westminster Abbey Muniments

INTRODUCTION

The purpose of this volume is to make available sources for the study of the church in London during the last quarter of the fourteenth century. It contains three distinct groups of material. The first consists of six documents (**1–395**) concerned with the clerical taxes of the years 1379–81 (Public Record Office E179 Clerical subsidies). The second is an assessment of ecclesiastical property in the city of London in 1392 (**396–546**, Corporation of London Records Office). The third consists of the *acta* of William Courtenay, bishop of London 1375–81 (**547–652**), collected from a variety of sources. The aim in gathering these *acta* has been to try to fill, in part, the gap left by the loss of his register. In furtherance of this aim the registers of contemporary bishops, the cartularies of religious houses in the diocese, and certain classes of Public Records have been examined. Some documents yielded by this investigation are in London repositories but the majority are to be found in local record offices from Durham to Exeter, and from Hereford to Norwich.

Taxation of the clergy, 1379–81
By the beginning of our period taxation of the clergy was long-established. The property of the English church was assessed for taxation purposes by order of pope Nicholas IV in about 1291,[1] and this assessment was utilized by the crown when it too imposed taxes on the clergy. After 1291 there had been only two grants, and after 1335 none, of clerical taxes to the crown which were not based on the 1291 *Taxatio*.[2] Grants made by the clergy of the two provinces in their convocations were collected by means of machinery already well-established before the mid-fourteenth century[3] and the yield of a tenth from Canterbury province was £16,000.[4] Since 1291 the authority and value of the assessment had been undermined in a number of ways. From the crown's point of view there were, by the 1370s, three chief drawbacks: the exemptions granted from these taxes; the fact that property given to the church since 1291 was not included; and, above all, the fact that the *Taxatio* did not cover the many unbeneficed clergy who received their payment not from endowments of property, but from stipends.

The decade 1371 to 1381 was a period of experiment in the taxation of the clergy, as indeed it was also of the laity. As far as the clergy were concerned, the crown was basically attempting to exploit the untapped source of revenue represented by their incomes. That the unbeneficed were not

---

1. *Taxatio*.
2. D. B. Weske, *Convocation of the Clergy* (1937), appendices A and B, and *C.F.R.*
3. 'The collectors of clerical subsidies granted to the king by the English clergy', *The English Government at Work*, ii, ed. W. A. Morris and J. R. Strayer (1947).
4. M. McKisack, *The Fourteenth Century* (1959), 287.

represented in convocation[5] seems to have been no stumbling block to the authorities. In 1371 convocation, under pressure from parliament, granted to the crown the sum of £50,000 to be collected in a year, a sum far greater than the clergy were accustomed to pay. The tax was a failure; it aroused widespread opposition and its yield was disappointing. The next experiment, in 1377, was a poll tax with two rates of payment: every beneficed person, regular or secular, was to pay 1s 0d, and every other cleric over fourteen years of age and not a mendicant was to pay 4d.

The first of the experimental taxes from which lists of names survive for London diocese was the poll tax of 1379. The first stage in the granting of this tax was a royal writ of 16 March 1379 sent to Simon Sudbury, archbishop of Canterbury, directing him to summon a meeting of convocation. This he did in a mandate dated 21 March; Courtenay directed it to the other bishops on 31 March (606). The meeting, which took place in St Paul's cathedral, began on 9 May, and there was continuous discussion until 23 May when the grant was made.[6] The tax was of exceptional complexity and sophistication, for there were to be fifteen rates of payment according to rank and income, ranging from the archbishop of Canterbury assessed at 10 marks (£6 13s 4d) to unbeneficed clerks at 4d each. Bishops, including Courtenay, were to pay 6 marks (£4), while chaplains, so numerous in the city of London, were to pay 2s 0d.[7] Sudbury notified the crown of the grant on 6 June 1379,[8] and on the same day writs ordering collection were issued. Collectors' names were to be certified to the exchequer by the bishops before 24 June, and the money was to be delivered in two equal portions by 7 July and 8 September.[9]

Among the duties of the collectors specified in the writs enjoining appointment was that, when accounting at the exchequer, they should certify the names and status of all the clergy who had to contribute to the tax. One such certificate, containing particulars of the account of the collectors within the city and suburbs of London, is the first document in this volume (1–117). The certificate consists of a narrow roll of twelve membranes, setting out the names of the contributing clergy first by religious houses (1–17), and then by parishes grouped in alphabetical order (18–110), and adding some miscellaneous items (111–14). At this point another hand takes over, giving a further twelve names, mostly of celebrants and subclerks in parish churches (115). Finally, in a third hand, comes the assessment of the hospital of St Katherine by the Tower, and the names of further chaplains (116–17). These 'appendices' may be explained in either of two ways. They may represent those who, undiscovered or overlooked at the assessors' first visitation, were yet detected at the second, for there is some evidence, at least among the activities of collectors of lay subsidies, that assessors were wont to make more than one visit.[10] The other possibility is that the collectors were supplied by their bishop with a list of clergy to be

5. B. Putnam, 'Maximum wage-laws for priests after the Black Death, 1348–1381', *American Historical Review*, xxi (1915–16), 15.
6. Reg. Sudbury (Cant.) ff.53, 55.
7. The rates are set out in *C.F.R. 1377–83*, 139–40.
8. Reg. Sudbury (Cant.) f.55v.
9. E179/35/8 addressed to the bishop of Lincoln.
10. R. H. Hilton, *The English Peasantry in the Later Middle Ages* (1975), 32.

taxed, which they found in the course of their duties to be incomplete. Such was the case in Lincoln diocese in 1381 when the collector in the archdeaconries of Lincoln and Stow discovered twenty-two tax-payers not on the bishop's roll.[11]

Another tax with experimental features was levied from the clergy of the southern province in 1380. The taxation process was set in motion by a royal request for convocation, dated 2 December 1379, which was answered the following day when Sudbury issued his mandate ordering attendance. This was forwarded by Courtenay to the other bishops on 12 December (**619**). The meeting, which took place in St Paul's cathedral, began on 4 February 1380 and was still in session on 29 February when the grant was made. This tax was to be paid at the rate of 16d in the mark – that is, a tenth – on all benefices already assessed in 1291, and 16d in the mark on two-thirds of the value of benefices not assessed. Unbeneficed priests, advocates, registrars, proctors and notaries were to pay 2s 0d each. Sudbury's notification of the grant was dated 6 March.[12] On the same day, the crown issued the writ ordering collection of the tax; it was to be levied even from the exempt, the privileged, and the members of royal free chapels. The terms were 3 May and 24 June, when equal portions were to be paid, and the names of collectors were to be certified to the exchequer before 23 April. Courtenay notified the barons of the exchequer on 10 April of his choice of collectors (**628**).

This tax was a hybrid, combining as it did the 1291 assessment, a new assessment of less well-endowed benefices, and a poll tax on unbeneficed personnel. The three features appear to have been kept separate by the collectors in London diocese when returning their particulars of account to the exchequer; there survives a list, giving the *beneficia minuta* only, returned by the abbot of Stratford Langthorn and the priors of Dunmow and Royston.[13] Even more conclusive is the evidence from the city and archdeaconry of London for here the three distinct lists survive: the assessed benefices; the *beneficia minuta*[14] on the dorse of the same document; and a list of those paying the poll tax of 2s 0d (**118–39**). The names of the chaplains and other unbeneficed clergy are contained on a single sheet of parchment, on which the list is arranged in two columns on both face and dorse. It shows that 400 ecclesiastical persons in the archdeaconry paid 2s 0d, and forms a useful complement to the particulars of 1379; it is, however, less precise, because the men are not assigned to parishes, and less detailed, because a higher proportion appear without surnames.

Finally, we come to the documents arising from the notorious poll tax of 1381. A royal writ of 28 September 1380 ordered a meeting of convocation to take place as soon as possible in the church of All Saints, Northampton, and consequently Sudbury issued a mandate on 4 October. Courtenay relayed it to the other bishops on 18 October (**637**). The meeting began on 1 December, and on 5 December the clergy, protesting that their grant was not to be used as a precedent, conceded a poll tax of 6s 8d a head. From

11. E179/35/22d.
12. Reg. Sudbury (Cant.) ff.59v–60.
13. E179/42/6.
14. E179/42/5.

this imposition there were to be no exceptions, even the exempt and the privileged were to pay, since all beneficed clergy, regulars and seculars alike, of whatever rank or sex, had to contribute, but 'in such a way that the better off should support the poorer'.[15]

More information is contained in a writ of 20 December 1380 which ordered collection. The terms were to be 22 February and 24 June 1381, and the collectors' names were to be certified to the exchequer by 2 February. The writ went on to give each bishop wide powers of discretion over the way in which they collected the tax (**640**). Two days later, Sudbury, availing himself of the scope allowed him in the royal writ, wrote to advise his bishops on the method of collection. The bishop should send his mandate to each archdeacon or his official, the cathedral church, and any exempt jurisdictions in the diocese, ordering that on a day named they should certify to him the names of all dignitaries, clergy, and monks, of whatever rank, beneficed, unbeneficed, exempt, and privileged. On that day the archdeacons or their officials, and two canons of the cathedral if it were secular (otherwise two sufficient clergy of the diocese) and one rector from each deanery, were to report to the bishop the names of all contributors and the amounts they would pay. It is clear that, in addition, Sudbury envisaged another grade of payment of 3s 4d for the unbeneficed, and for regulars and nuns below the rank of prior,[16] and, as the London material demonstrates, this grade was utilized. Early in 1381, on 11 January, Courtenay issued one, and possibly all, his commissions to collectors (**640**).

From the operation of this poll tax four documents remain which throw light on the personnel of the London city and diocesan clergy at this time. First, William Coleyn's particulars of account (**140–72**) which cover the cathedral clergy, about whom nothing survives for the 1379 or 1380 taxes. Secondly, a fragment of the assessment of the city of London clergy (**173–202**) which is similar in scope and arrangement to the 1379 material. The third document (**203–16**), though covering part of the city of London, does not originate in the diocese, for it concerns those thirteen parishes scattered about the city which formed the deanery of Bow and came within the peculiar jurisdiction of the archbishop of Canterbury. This is the most precise and detailed of all the taxation documents. The fourth document contains the particulars for the archdeaconry of Middlesex (**217–395**), an area which covered not only the county of Middlesex but also a part of Hertfordshire (the deanery of Braughing) and of Essex (the deaneries of Hedingham, Dunmow, and Harlow).

Despite the order that even the exempt and privileged were to pay this tax, seemingly some exceptions were admitted after all. The minoresses of Aldgate had been given exemption from all clerical taxes by Edward III, and they were excused payment of the 1380 tax, as evidence from Lincoln diocese shows. In 1381 a letter of 1 March addressed to the collectors in the city of London confirmed their exemption.[17] The clergy of the royal free chapel of St Martin le Grand were also exonerated after a spirited protest by their

15. Reg. Sudbury (Cant.) f.72v.
16. L.A.O. Reg. 12B ff.32–34. *The Anonimalle Chronicle*, ed. V. H. Galbraith (1927), 132–3 also mentions this grade of 3s 4d.
17. *C.C.R. 1377–81*, 502; E179/35/12; E179/42/8 no. 1.

dean mr Walter Skirlaw. A note at the foot of the writ of exemption records that the grant was made with the assent of mr John Codeford, official of the bishop of London.[18]

The evidence of the particulars of account (**140–395**) shows that two of the other injunctions of the writ, that the rich were to help the poorer, and that the bishops should raise the tax in the manner they saw fit, were carried out. Indeed, from this sample it seems that in every collecting area the method of making up the required total was slightly different. William Coleyn, collector in St Paul's and its immediate jurisdiction, first raised 6s 8d from all the beneficed men on his list. From nearly half of the un-beneficed clergy he exacted sums on a sliding scale whose highest rate was 5s 4d (**142–3**), but from many of the other unbeneficed clergy of St Paul's he levied only 3s 4d (**144–5**). He then raised supplementary sums not only from the beneficed whose names were included on the first list, but from others whose names had not occurred earlier. Many of these were pre-bendaries (**146–8**), minor canons or chantry priests (**149–50**), whose role as 'supplementaries' only, may well be explained by the fact that many, if not all, were pluralists who paid their main contribution elsewhere, and whose St Paul's income was used to help make up the cathedral's required total sum.

The collectors in London evidently had two rolls, the surviving one showing that 3s 4d was exacted from each person above the rank of clerk. The second roll doubtless showed how the required sum of £210 6s 8d was exacted, so that the grand total (**202**) actually showed a small surplus. Within the deanery of Bow a clear distinction was observed between per-petual chaplains, namely those with a benefice, and the ordinary chaplains, the clerical casual labouring class. The former paid 6s 8d, the latter 3s 4d, and the deficit was made up by taxing the thirteen rectors at about the rate of three-tenths.[19] The collectors in Middlesex archdeaconry charged chap-lains and celebrants at a standard rate of 3s 4d but usually took larger sums from incumbents whom they taxed at a rate which owed nothing to the 1291 assessment. Even so, the target of 6s 8d each was not reached until the exaction of £14 13s 4d from the abbot of Westminster gave the collectors a slight surplus.

From the evidence of these four documents it may be inferred that the great majority of the unbeneficed paid only 3s 4d each. And it is not un-likely that variations in collecting practice within the small geographical area under review may have led to jealousy and ill-feeling among the clergy of different jurisdictions.

The first question which arises about the value of the assessments con-cerns their completeness as a series of 'clerical censuses'. Here several com-ments may be offered. First, since the lists were compiled for taxation purposes the possibility of evasion must be borne in mind. Secondly, the

18. 18 May 1381, E179/42/8, no. 2.
19. In 1291 the eleven wealthiest rectories paid a total tax of £6 2s 8d; the two *beneficia minuta* were together worth £3, of which a tenth is 6s 0d, giving a total of £6 8s 8d (*Taxatio*, 19b, 20b). St John the Evangelist and St Mary Bothaw were not included in the 1291 assessment. The total value of the rectors' contribution in 1381 was £17 6s 8d.

collectors did not include in their particulars, mendicants, who were exempt from taxation, nor hospitallers, who paid with the laity. Thirdly, from any particular list some parishes are absent because they lay in the immediate jurisdiction of an authority other than that of the archdeacon. Fourthly, some small London hospitals are missing, but these are always elusive institutions, and usually poor. Bishops had the right to request that houses (and, indeed, parish benefices) might be exempt from a particular tax because of poverty, and had Courtenay's 'requests for exemption' survived some gaps might be explained. Conversely, pluralism must also be taken into account, though for a period when a very restricted number of Christian names was used and when the spelling of surnames was not standardised, it is difficult to quantify this factor precisely. Thus any conclusions about the number of clergy at a given time in a particular place, especially in London, can be only approximate.

Nevertheless the material is of great interest for the detailed information it provides about an important section of the community. Though comparatively reticent about the names of heads of religious houses (an exception is found in **116** which adds a new name to the *V.C.H.* list), and parochial incumbents (except **174–92, 203–15**), the assessments enable the tenure of office of some dozen prebendaries of St Paul's to be fixed with more precision than hitherto (**146–8**), and they designate as *magistri* seven men not listed by Dr Emden.[20]

Above all, the materials are informative about chaplains, an elusive class, but one whose great numbers constituted a distinctive feature of the late-medieval English church. At once a contrast is evident between the city and other parts of the diocese. Indeed the pattern would appear, from comparisons of London with Lincoln and Canterbury dioceses, to be very similar over much of rural England. The city of London, however, was unique for, while there were concentrations of chaplains in certain provincial towns (seventy-five in Lincoln and fifty-eight in Boston in 1380),[21] such numbers do not compare with the 497 or so who were in London in 1379.

Within this class several distinctions may be observed. There were parochial chaplains (e.g. **18**), fraternity chaplains (e.g. **45**), private chaplains (e.g. **32**), and most numerous of all, chantry chaplains. Chantry chaplains might be either cantarists or stipendiary mass-priests. Cantarists served perpetual chantries which were formally established with statutes, patrons, and endowments from which the chaplains were paid.[22] These chaplaincies were ecclesiastical benefices to which presentations were often recorded in episcopal registers. On the other hand, stipendiary mass-priests were hired for short periods. The need for such men arose because many people, when making their wills, directed that masses should be said for their souls after death. Such testators might leave a specific sum of money, name a certain number of masses, or direct that masses were to be said over a given length of time. The founding of a perpetual chantry demanded exceptional re-

20. Six were canons of St Martin le Grand (**16**); the seventh (**53**) was the official of the archdeacon of London (cf. Bodl. Libr. MS Film 651 ff. 68–68v).
21. E179/35/16 mm. 1, 10.
22. K. L. Wood-Legh, *Perpetual Chantries in Britain* (1965).

sources, but among those who could not afford, or did not wish, such a luxury were many Londoners whose provision for masses was generous, and thus many mass-priests were needed to fulfil their bequests. Which of the chantry chaplains were cantarists, and which mass-priests cannot, in many cases, be discovered. However, the compilers of **203–15** distinguished between perpetual chaplains paying 6s 8d, of whom there were thirteen, and chaplains paying 3s 4d, of whom there were seventy-six. We should probably envisage a similar ratio elsewhere in the city.

The smaller group, the cantarists, were investigated, for the period of Robert Braybrooke's episcopate (1381–1404) by Professor Rosalind Hill, who pointed out the bad press chantry priests had received from poets and prelates alike. She found no evidence that they flocked to London in such numbers that country parishes were bereft of pastors; and she concluded that, once inducted, they held their positions for some years and were not frequent exchangers; and, moreover, that their benefices were often inadequately endowed.[23] Inadequate endowment must be the excuse for the wide incidence of pluralism among the cantarists of St Paul's (**149–50**); many can be shown to have held benefices elsewhere, so giving credence to Chaucer's jibe about priests who neglected parish duties to serve a chantry in the cathedral.[24]

The cantarists are well-documented compared with the mass-priests, for these clerical casual labourers held no established benefices and consequently their appointments, resignations and conditions of service were not recorded for future reference. Our evidence shows, however, that there was a high degree of mobility among them (compare **40, 66–7, 72–86, 88–9** with **173–92**), and that, as might be expected from the nature of their employment, they formed an unstable element in the clerical population. The taxation particulars also suggest, they can do no more, that the clerical population of London was declining very slightly in the period 1379–81, a decline almost certainly due to a shrinkage in the number of stipendiaries. Even so, there were still many mass-priests and this numerous, mobile, and hard-to-discipline group must have been not only a matter of concern to the ecclesiastical authorities but also a prominent feature of London life at the time. It may be suggested that it was these men, rather than the less numerous cantarists, who were the object of attack by clergy and laymen alike.

Ecclesiastical property in the city of London, 1392
The document (**396–546**) consists of eleven membranes stitched at the head. Though it has no heading one may deduce, from both internal and external evidence, the time and circumstances which produced it. It appears to be a result of Richard II's quarrel with London, and, in particular, of the corporate fine of £100,000 laid on the city in the summer of 1392. Though this fine was pardoned, another of £10,000 was imposed in its stead. The assessment, it is contended, was made by the city authorities when attempting to

23. Rosalind Hill, '*A Chaunterie for Soules*: London chantries in the reign of Richard II', *Reign of Richard II*, 242–55.
24. *Reg. Sudbury (London)* index; *Canterbury Tales*, Prologue, 11. 509–10.

raise £100,000 (or perhaps £10,000) to placate the crown.[25] It would seem
to have been this attempt which resulted in petitions to the parliament of
1394 from two groups of Londoners: widows and clergy. The clergy's petition describes in some detail a new financial burden placed upon them. They
had been accustomed, they said, to pay only those taxes granted by the
clergy and commons for the realm's common profit; however, the mayor
and aldermen had imposed a new tax on all tenements and rents belonging
to benefices and churches in the city and suburbs, at the rate of 40d in the
pound.[26]

This description accords well with the document under discussion: it
cannot be reconciled with any known grant made by convocation; its scope
and arrangement, above all, its division into wards, point to a civil, rather
than an ecclesiastical origin; and beside the assessed sum for every item
there is in a right-hand column another figure, one sixth of the first amount,
making a rate of 40d in the pound. We may, therefore, assign this roll to
some period between the imposition of a large fine upon the city, about
mid-summer 1392, and the opening of the parliament at which the petition
was presented, in January 1394. Moreover, it may be suggested that the
early part of the period, the second half of 1392, is the most likely time for
the roll to have been drawn up. The assessment, as was said, is arranged by
wards. One ward, Cordwainer, is missing; another, Candlewick Street,
appears twice. Differences in arrangement and presentation of information
indicate that a different assessor was at work in each ward.

The document has no parallels among the records of ecclesiastical taxation. Not only its form, but the fact that the assessment was organised by
secular authority, make it unique. For the historian, the roll has a variety of
uses. In the first place, it provides information about the endowments of
ecclesiastical institutions of all kinds: parish churches, whose funding is
still somewhat obscure,[27] fraternities, chantries, religious houses and secular
colleges. The parish churches are those of London, but the religious houses
whose property was listed sometimes lay as far away as Croxton, Woburn,
or Chichester. The same is true of collegiate churches: Shottesbrooke,
Kingston-on-Thames, and two, if not three, Oxford colleges had property
in the city. Investigators of particular establishments will wish to compare
the information given here with deeds, rentals and cartularies where these
exist.[28]

In the second place, the assessment provides much information about the
owning and holding of property in the city. Here, as tenants or landlords,
may be found laymen of every rank (especially leading merchants), women,
and clergy of different grades including individual religious. The document

25. C. M. Barron, 'The quarrel of Richard II with London 1392–7', *Reign of Richard II*, 189–95.
26. *Rot. Parl.* iii, 325.
27. C. N. L. Brooke and G. Keir, *London 800–1216* (1975), 126.
28. See e.g., *Cartulary of St Mary Clerkenwell*, ed. W. O. Hassall (Camden third series, lxxi, 1949); *The Cartulary of Holy Trinity Aldgate*, ed. G. A. J. Hodgett (L.R.S. vii, 1971); J. Watney, *Some Account of the Hospital of St Thomas of Acon* (1892); *The Cartulary of St Bartholomew's Hospital*, ed. N. J. M. Kerling (1973); *Chartulary of the Hospital of St Thomas the Martyr Southwark*, anon. (1932); Merton College Catalogue of Manuscripts vol. ix (National Register of Archives).

raises problems, for it is often ambiguous and the exact interest of institutions and individuals in a particular property is unclear. Nevertheless, the roll provides evidence of a most striking kind about the interconnection between laity and clergy at a financial level, an interconnection which explains the intervention of the city authorities in tithe disputes during the next century.[29]

In the third place, the assessment offers guidance to the student of the topography of medieval London in a number of ways: by indicating commercial areas, through its references to clusters of shops (e.g., **415–16, 432, 437, 450, 457–8, 460, 522**); by its reference to locations, sometimes precisely given (e.g., **411, 436, 445, 459, 506–7**); above all, by the way in which property belonging to one establishment is scattered among the entries for one ward or even for a single parish. This suggests that the entries, though apparently arranged haphazardly, were in fact collected, and then set down, on a topographical basis.

Acta of William Courtenay, bishop of London, 1375–81

The collection of Courtenay's *acta* (**547–652**) makes no claim to be a reconstruction of his lost register.[30] The register, if it followed the usual pattern, would have been divided into sections according to types of business; it would have contained letters addressed to the bishop; and other categories of records conspicuously absent from the material gathered here, namely, institutions not involving exchanges, ordinations, and memoranda of all kinds. The registered *acta* would have been contemporary copies. The majority of the *acta* printed here are also contemporary copies, but the collection includes also twenty original *acta*, all but one in the P.R.O., five copies made later in the middle ages, and one eighteenth-century copy. The collected *acta* are printed in chronological order but many of them fall into well-defined classes: those concerning the exchange of benefices; letters written in the course of contacts between the royal and episcopal administrations; documents arising from provincial business; texts concerning relations with the papacy and acts issued as a consequence of the geographical position of the diocese. Brief comments may be offered on each group in turn.

The largest group of *acta* arose from the practice, widespread by the end of the fourteenth century, of exchanging benefices. These letters are of two kinds: commissions to other bishops to effect exchanges, and certificates of execution of similar commissions addressed to Courtenay. Such material must have formed a part of the institutions section of the lost register, but how large a proportion must remain conjectural. During Sudbury's tenure of the see, exchanges accounted for over 45 per cent of institutions, the majority, 239 out of 332, being exchanges with benefices outside the dio-

---

29. J. A. F. Thomson, 'Tithe disputes in later medieval London', *English Historical Review*, lxxviii (1963), 1–17.

30. It is not known when Courtenay's register of acts as bishop of London disappeared. The register of his successor, Robert Braybrooke, includes two of Courtenay's *acta* (Guildhall Library MS 9531/3 ff. 282v–3, 378v–9) but these may have been copied from the originals. Courtenay's was not among the other London registers by the time Matthew Hutton made his transcripts (B.L. Harl. MS 6955) c. 1686.

cese.[31] Sudbury's manipulation of the exchange system to increase the amount of patronage at his disposal was certainly in contrast to the practice of Braybrooke[32] and may well have contrasted with that of Courtenay whose later fulmination on this subject is familiar. While such exchanges await a full-scale study[33] we may note here that the practice greatly increased the contacts between episcopal chanceries, and it may be speculated whether such contacts increased to any great extent the mobility of ecclesiastical administrators.

The letters arising from the interaction between royal and episcopal administration form the second largest group. Co-operation between the two powers is shown, firstly, by the way in which the church performed services for the lay courts (**558, 615**). Secondly, it appeared in the part played by secular authority in punishing offenders against ecclesiastical law. The process by which the church enlisted the help of the lay arm[34] was set in motion by a signification of excommunication addressed to the chancery. Fifteen of Courtenay's significations have survived, but this is less than the original number. The Patent Rolls refer to one of his significations not now extant,[35] and probably others have been lost, for, to take one example, there are no significations of obdurate excommunicates in the archdeaconry of Middlesex. Noteworthy among the significations are two concerning miscreants living, temporarily or permanently, in parishes within the city of London (**571, 579**); both are careful to state that the parish was 'within our jurisdiction' thus forestalling any allegation that the parish was in the deanery of Bow and so outside Courtenay's diocese.

Almost invariably the crime which caused the sentence was contumacy. In three cases the culprits had failed to appear before the president of the consistory of London (**571–3**), in one before the bishop's commissary (**608**), and in another before the bishop himself (**613**). A comparison with evidence from other dioceses suggests that the thirteen incumbents listed in **652** had originally been proceeded against for non-payment of clerical taxes. The obdurates in the sample of significations included laymen and a laywoman as well as clergy. Among the seventeen clerical culprits the most distinguished was mr Nicholas Chaddesden (**555**), who seems to have clashed with Courtenay's commissaries in a case which arose from the visitation of St Bartholomew's hospital.[36] But the most celebrated was the chaplain John Ball (**611**). An itinerant preacher of great power, he had already been in trouble with several members of the episcopate before Courtenay signified him as excommunicate in 1379.[37] Ball was later to achieve notoriety in the

31. *Reg. Sudbury (London)*, i, p. viii.
32. Butler, 'Braybrooke', i, 227.
33. See, meanwhile, R. L. Storey, 'Ecclesiastical causes in Chancery', *The Study of Medieval Records*, ed. D. A. Bullough and R. L. Storey (1971), 236–59.
34. F. D. Logan, *Excommunication and the Secular Arm in Medieval England* (Toronto, 1968).
35. *C.P.R. 1374–7*, 333.
36. *Ibid.*, 216; Historical Manuscripts Commission *9th Report*, Appendix i, 44a; Emden, *Oxford*, i, 380–1.
37. Ball had previously appeared before Simon Islip archbishop of Canterbury, William Bateman bishop of Norwich, Michael Northburgh bishop of London, and had been excommunicated by John Buckingham bishop of Lincoln (L.A.O. Reg. 12 f. 94).

Peasants' Revolt.[38] A third example of obduracy calls for comment. The continuing use of the caption as a legal instrument is usually regarded as the best indication of its effectiveness. But more immediately impressive is the evidence provided by the case of Ralph Daventry. A clerk of London diocese, he was twice signified as obdurate by his bishop early in February 1377 (**572–3**). Within a month he had been arrested, imprisoned at Stafford, had appealed to Rome, and to the court of Canterbury for protection, and had petitioned the crown for his release. This was granted in an order to the sheriff of Stafford on 8 March.[39]

The third aspect of church-state relations illustrated by these *acta* is the taxation of the clergy, already discussed above. Taxation was a subject closely linked with provincial business, for it was voted at meetings of the convocations of the two provinces. In the organisation of meetings of the Canterbury convocation the bishop of London, in his role of dean of the province,[40] played an essential part. He relayed the orders of the archbishop to the other suffragans (**553, 568, 582, 606, 619, 637**), and his reports on this task were sometimes recorded *in extenso* in the proceedings of convocation (**585, 621, 639**). Other archiepiscopal letters transmitted by Courtenay as bishop of London included orders for the saying of prayers for patriotic purposes (**566**), and the final reissue of the constitution *Effrenata* aimed at curbing clerical wages (**617**).[41] Courtenay performed a like task in connection with papal and curial documents since these were promulgated on a provincial basis. Thus Sudbury and Courtenay were responsible for circularising a papal bull (**607**) issued in the course of the propaganda war early in the schism,[42] as well as requests for procurations for papal nuncios (**554, 576, 578**).[43]

The bishop of London occupied his special place in provincial administration because of the geographical location of his see. This location also gave him contacts with his fellow-bishops unconnected with archiepiscopal mandates, for English prelates, with the exception of the bishop of Winchester and the archbishop of Canterbury, had London houses in which, on occasion, they wished to conduct episcopal business. To do so they required the permission of the bishop of London, and four of Courtenay's licences to episcopal colleagues have been found (**593, 622, 624, 641**), survivors of a class which doubtless was once considerable. Thomas Brantingham bishop of Exeter, for example, celebrated orders in the chapel of his London house on at least three occasions before the licence printed here was issued. Each time he did so by Courtenay's permission, as the record in his register was careful to state.[44] Possibly **593** was registered in full because of the wide powers it conveyed. How wide these powers were may be seen by comparing this licence with **624**, issued to the bishop of Hereford. The dif-

38. *Chronicon Angliae*, ed. E. M. Thompson (Rolls Series, 1874), 320–2.
39. *C.C.R. 1374–7*, 548.
40. I. J. Churchill, *Canterbury Administration*, i (1933), 355–9.
41. B. Putnam, 'Maximum wage-laws for priests after the Black Death, 1348–1381', *American Historical Review*, xxi (1915–16), 12–32.
42. E. Perroy, *L'Angleterre et le grand schisme d'occident* (1933), 63.
43. W. E. Lunt, *Financial Relations of the Papacy with England 1327–1534* (Cambridge, Mass., 1962), 678, 680–1.
44. Reg. Brantingham ii ff. 45(2), 47.

ference between the two licences is probably to be explained not by Brant-ingham's long-standing friendship with Courtenay[45] but by the fact that his duties as treasurer kept him in London for considerable periods. He had to conduct much of his diocesan administration, such as the approving or rejecting of elections to the headships of religious houses (**622, 641**), from his London inn.

While some of the *acta* already mentioned have political overtones, for example, those connected with taxation, prayers for peace, and with the schism, a small number may be considered as wholly political in content. Two *acta*, one undated, arose from Courtenay's defence of Wykeham when his colleague of Winchester was in disgrace in 1376–7 (**569–70**).[46] A third resulted from a spectacular violation of the sanctuary of Westminster abbey, in which two men were killed; the culprits were excommunicated by Sud-bury, and the sentence was notified to the rest of the bench by Courtenay (**595**) and published by him, *terribiliter*, at St Paul's.[47] The last of the political *acta* was the denunciation, by the prior of Christ Church Canter-bury, guardian of the spiritualities of the archbishopric *sede vacante*, of those who murdered Simon Sudbury during the Peasants' Revolt (**650**).

Though the *acta* tell us little about religion in the diocese of London at this time, they do throw light on two aspects of Courtenay's diocesan administration: his movements and his subordinates. By using the dating clauses of the *acta* and by adding other references to his whereabouts, for example, in the rolls of parliament, and in documents issued by his sub-ordinates while he was outside the diocese, it is possible to make an outline of his itinerary from the day of his profession of obedience as bishop of London, to his appearance in parliament as 'former bishop of London, elect of Canterbury'.

After taking his oath of obedience at the bishop of Winchester's manor of Esher, Surrey, on 1 December 1375,[48] Courtenay moved towards London for on 5 December he transacted business at Barnes. He appears next on 8 March 1376 at Cowick, Devon, probably on a visit to his family. His absence from London seems to have been protracted for Adam Mottrum acted as vicar-general in spirituals on 10 and 25 February and 19 March. Courtenay was back in London for the opening of parliament on 28 April, and he was there during the early summer (5, 29 May; 8, 21, 25, 26 June; 1, 10 July). On 20 July he transacted business at his manor of Stepney, but in the late autumn he was again in London, mostly at his palace by St Paul's (23, 27 October; 2, 5 November). Christmas, it would seem, he spent at his Essex manor of Wickham; at least we know he was there on 23 December. Courtenay was in London on 20 January 1377, attended both parliament and convocation that winter, and conducted business, mostly in his palace, on 4, 8, 9 and 22 February and 6 March. He was absent from the diocese on 9 May 1377 but intermittently through the summer he is known to have

45. Reg. Courtenay (Heref.) f. 8v; Reg. Brantingham ii ff. **23**, 24v second sequence.
46. M. McKisack, *The Fourteenth Century* (1959), 394–6.
47. *Ibid.*, 403–4; Thomas Walsingham, *Historia Anglicana*, ed. H. T. Riley, i (Rolls Series, 1863), 379.
48. See the dating clauses of the *acta* **547–652**, and *Rot. Parl.* ii, 321–2, 361; iii, 3–4, 32, 55–6, 71–2, 88–9, 98; Reg. Sudbury (Cant.) ff. 33v, 55, 59v, 72.

conducted business in London (14, 30 June; 25 July; 7 August). He was in London and Fulham (10 October), at Westminster for parliament (13 October), and, as far as can be ascertained, he remained at London and Fulham to the end of the year (London 3 November; Fulham 9, 11 December; London 16 December).

The following year, 1378, is ill-documented but in the first seven months it is recorded that the bishop was at Fulham on 9 and 31 January; 5 and 18 February; and 2 July, and in London on 28 August and 26 September, and then he went to Gloucester for the October parliament. He had returned to London by 29 November. Christmas was probably spent at Wickham, and from the dates recorded (16 December 1378; 20, 28 January 1379) it appears that he stayed there until the end of January. In March he transacted business at Fulham on several occasions (12, 16, 29, 31 March). He attended the parliament which began on 24 April, transacted business at Fulham on 4 May, but was back at St Paul's for convocation on 9 May. He remained in his palace by the cathedral towards the end of the month (20, 23 May), and is found at Fulham in June (16, 22 June). This year, 1379, is the first of his episcopate in which Courtenay can be seen to make a summer stay at one of his country manors, for he left London early in July and apparently spent the rest of the month at Wickham (London 1 July; Wickham 6, 10, 27 July). The cause of his leaving London may well have been the plague which broke out again that year.[49] He was in London in September (4, 13 September), and this was followed by an apparently protracted stay at Wickham (10 November; 12, 23 December).

After Christmas at Wickham, Courtenay was back at Fulham on the last day of 1379, doubtless in preparation for the opening of parliament which he attended on 16 January 1380. He was present also at the opening of convocation on 4 February, but at the remaining sessions he was represented by a proctor. In February, March and April 1380 he was to be found in or near London (Fulham 12 February; London 17 February; Fulham 5 March; London 8, 20 March, 10, 21 April; Westminster palace 28 April). During the next three months nothing is known for certain of his movements, but he was outside the diocese on 11 May when John Codeford, vicar-general, transacted business on his behalf. August and parts of September again found him in or near London (London 4 August; Fulham 10 August; London 6, 30 September), but on 25 September he was away from his diocese. That winter both parliament and convocation met at Northampton, and it is known that Courtenay was there in the interval between the two meetings. This may well have meant that his stay lasted a month, from the opening of parliament (5 November) to the last day of convocation (6 December). By 18 December he was back at Fulham.

The following year, 1381, Courtenay was at 'Langeley', possibly Kings Langley, Hertfordshire, on 11 January. On 10 February he was in London, and on 5 March at Fulham. From then onwards, until his translation, Courtenay's surviving letters are dated from London (6, 12, 21 March; 2 May; 18 August). Letters issued by his vicars-general, John Codeford on 18 May and Adam Mottrum on 7 June, show, however, that he made two excursions outside the diocesan boundaries, and suggest that he was out of

49. E. L. Sabine, 'Butchering in medieval London', *Speculum*, viii (1933), 348.

the city at the height of the Peasants' Revolt. Translated to Canterbury on 9 September Courtenay nevertheless issued documents as bishop of London on 16 September and 3 October. On 19 October he transacted business in the bishop of Worcester's house outside Temple Bar, which suggests that he may already have relinquished his London houses; on 3 November Courtenay appeared in parliament as 'former bishop of London'.

Some tentative conclusions may be drawn from the itinerary. It is noteworthy that none of the documents here cited was dated from Much Hadham, the Hertfordshire manor house which was the favourite residence of Courtenay's successor. Courtenay's favourite country manor was Wickham where he spent three Christmases and where he imparked 300 acres of land under a royal licence granted on 16 January 1377.[50] Membership of the council from July 1377 to October 1378 probably confined Courtenay to the neighbourhood of London;[51] release from this burden meant more time at Wickham. The bishop of London was also well supplied with houses near the capital and he spent much time in his palace next to the cathedral; when going further afield his preference for Fulham rather than Stepney is unmistakeable.

Just as the dating clauses of the *acta* allow glimpses of Courtenay's movements so some information about his subordinates may be gleaned from other parts of the *acta*. From them as well as from other sources there can be discovered the names of seven men who were active in Courtenay's administration of the diocese. Thomas Neylonde, a non-graduate, was in Courtenay's employ at this time, but of him nothing is known save that he originated from Norwich diocese (**607**).

The names of five graduates in Courtenay's employment during his London years are known: Richard Warmyngton, John Codeford, John Lydford, Adam Mottrum, and John Prophet. Richard Warmyngton was one of the few of Sudbury's servants who remained in London diocese when his master moved on to Canterbury. A notary public, he was registrar of the consistory court of London in 1370.[52] During Courtenay's episcopate he was to be found acting both with and without his bishop in a series of land transactions connected with religious houses (**588**).[53] Courtenay's friendship with the lawyer John Codeford went back to their Oxford days.[54] Codeford had twice been commissioned a vicar-general of Courtenay at Hereford,[55] and he again acted in that capacity on three occasions in London (**630, 635, 647**). In addition, he was sometimes deputed as a special commissary, one letter written in that capacity having survived.[56] Codeford's death in 1381 or 1382 deprived Courtenay of an old friend and colleague whose service would have been valuable in Canterbury administration. Another man whose connection with Courtenay dated from Hereford,

50. *C.P.R. 1374–7*, 407.
51. N. B. Lewis, 'The "Continual Council" in the early years of Richard II, 1377–1380', *English Historical Review*, xli (1926), 246–51.
52. *Reg. Sudbury (London)* i, 182, 270n.
53. *C.P.R. 1374–7*, 125; *C.P.R. 1377–81*, 80, 219; *C.C.R. 1377–81*, 480; he was dead by 8 March 1379 (Reg. Sudbury (Cant.) f. 128).
54. Emden, *Oxford*, i, 453.
55. Reg. Courtenay (Heref.) ff. 3v, 5.
56. W.A.M. no. 5996.

if not from Oxford days, was John Lydford, whose memorandum book contains two of Courtenay's London *acta* (**569–70**). Lydford spent much of the early 1370s at the papal court in Avignon, and left Courtenay's service in 1377 to become official of the diocese of Winchester. He remained, however, on good terms with Courtenay whom he advised even from his 'retirement' at Exeter.[57] While Codeford and Lydford had both served Courtenay at Hereford, it is not known when Adam Mottrum joined his service. Mottrum is found acting as vicar-general at the beginning (**549–52**) as well as at the end (**648**) of the episcopate. He was Courtenay's London chancellor[58] and later performed the same service for him at Canterbury.[59] Finally, possibly the most distinguished of Courtenay's subordinates was John Prophet, a Welshman and notary who attested one of the *acta* (**607**), as well as an agreement issued jointly by the bishops of London, Ely, St Davids, Salisbury and Chichester on 1 July 1376.[60] Like Codeford and Lydford, Prophet had been in Courtenay's service at Hereford[61] and he continued to serve him at Canterbury for some years before becoming a king's clerk in the later 1380s.[62]

In addition to these six the identity of one other of Courtenay's clerical subordinates is known, that of a suffragan bishop who performed episcopal acts on his behalf,[63] but this total of seven can only have been a small proportion of the clerks who assisted the bishop in his diocesan administration. Courtenay's successor, Robert Braybrooke, usually maintained a staff of about twenty-five clerks, fifteen of whom lived in his household,[64] and this difference between the numbers known for Courtenay's episcopate and those known for Braybrooke's illustrates the difference in documentation between the two periods. Although it has to be admitted that we have evidence for a clearer picture of the diocese of London both before and after Courtenay's episcopate than during his own tenure of the see, the present collection of Courtenay's *acta* and the taxation lists of 1379–81 assembled in this volume should go some way to redress the balance.

Note on Editorial Method
In the following calendars the use of square brackets indicates editorial additions. Transcripts of words or phrases are contained in round brackets. Unidentified place-names are given in inverted commas. Italics are used to indicate marginalia. In **1–395** and **547–652** the title dominus (domina) used for all ecclesiastical persons above the rank of clerk has been omitted from the calendar. In **1–395** the names in square brackets have been supplied from the *V.C.H.* (in the case of heads of religious houses), R. Newcourt,

57. *John Lydford's Book*, 5–11.
58. *Ibid.*, no. 234.
59. Emden, *Cambridge*, 415.
60. *C.P.R. 1374–7*, 292.
61. Occurs as registrar of the consistory of Hereford 7 Feb. 1371 (Reg. Courtenay (Heref.) f. 6v).
62. Emden, *Oxford*, iii, 1523.
63. William Egmund 'Pisenensis' (Pissinessis or Prissinensis) (Essex Record Office D/DPr 148; *C.P.R. 1396–9*, 445). He later served the bishop of Lincoln (*Handbook of British Chronology*, ed. F. M. Powicke and E. B. Fryde, 2nd ed. (1961), 267).
64. Butler, 'Braybrooke', i, 253.

Repertorium Ecclesiasticum Parochiale Londinense (1708–10), and G. Hennessy, *Novum Repertorium Ecclesiasticum Parochiale Londinense* (1898).

Acknowledgements
Thanks are due to: the committee of the Royal Holloway College Association Jubilee Fellowship Research Fund for financial support during the preparation of this volume; Miss P. K. Crimmin and Dr J. P. Croft for advice and encouragement; and Dr L. H. Butler for making available his unpublished doctoral dissertation.

TAXATION OF THE CLERGY, 1379–81

POLL TAX OF 1379 IN THE CITY OF LONDON

1. [E179/42/4a m. 1] *London*. Particulars of account of Thomas de Kendale[1] rector of St Augustine Watling Street (at the Gate), Thomas [Pateshull] rector of St John Walbrook (Walbrok), John [Baud] rector of St Nicholas Cole Abbey (Coldeabbey) and Roger [Fryseby] rector of St Michael le Querne (ad Bladinum) collectors of a subsidy granted to the king by the prelates and clergy of Canterbury province in the second year of his reign from all ecclesiastical persons exempt and non-exempt in the city and suburbs of London except the cathedral of St Paul's London, as follows:

1. *de Kendale* interlined.

2. St Bartholomew Smithfield (Smethefeld). Prior [Thomas Watford] estimated at £333 6s 8d, paying £3.
Canons paying 3s 4d each: Andrew Halstede, John Raukdych, Richard Hexton, William Gydeney, John Dunmowe, John de Watford, John Kyllysby, John Spaldyngg, Philip Shalden, John Flete, Thomas Vury, Thomas Kyng, John Batayle, William Pyrye, John Yongge.
Clerks paying 4d each: John Mcryfeld, John Tennyngton, William Burton, Nicholas and Thomas clerks of the church, William clerk of the refectory, John Theobaud.
John Chyshull paying 2s.
Total £5 14s 4d.

3. Church of Holy Trinity Aldgate (within Aldgate). Prior [William de Rysyng] estimated at £333 6s 8d, paying £3.
Canons paying 3s 4d each: Ralph de Cantebregia, Robert de Exonia, John de Repton, John Passour, John de Oxonia, Henry Scherdelowe, John Benet, John More, John Neuton, John Braytoft, Richard Sarych, John Upton, John Bentyngford, Richard Rothyng, John Dene, William Bromlee, William Haredon.
Clerks paying 4d each: Thomas Huntyngdone, Thomas Lewconore, John Oxonie, John Hatfeld, William clerk of the rent-collector (reddituarii), Thomas Waterdone, Ralph clerk of John de Rypton.
Total £5 19s.

4. Hospital of St Mary without Bishopsgate (Byschopgate). Prior [John de Lyndeseye] estimated at £100, paying £1 10s.
Canons paying 1s 8d each: Thomas Compton, Robert Saxe, John Carlton, John Fulham, Thomas Wolnerch, John Lyce, Michael de la Rollys, Thomas Bradlee, Thomas Alvyrton, John Myldenhale, Thomas More.
Clerk paying 4d: Walter Broun.

Sisters paying 1s 8d each: Alice Croydon, Joan Lyndeseye, Christine
  Helpysfeld, Christine Redys, Agnes Walklyf, [m. 2] Katherine Whysch.
Total £2 18s 8d.

5. St HELEN WITHIN BISHOPSGATE. Prioress estimated at £100, paying £1
10s.
Nuns paying 1s 8d each: Margaret Lacer, Margaret Andrew, Isabel Poulee,
  Juliana Pole, Alice Doulee, Margaret Moreys, Alice Moreys, Katherine
  Wolf, Cecily Frensch, Agnes More, Joan Heyron.
Secular chaplains paying 2s each: Nicholas parochial chaplain, John con-
  ventual chaplain, John Fey, Hugh Banbery, John Fyschere, John Wat-
  forde, William Norhampton, William chaplain of the prioress.
Clerk paying 4d: Robert.
Total £3 4s 8d.

6. HALIWELL (Halywell). Prioress estimated at £53 6s 8d, paying 13s 4d.
Nuns paying 1s each: Isabel Notton, Helen Goshalme, Joan Hyde, Joan
  Parker, Isabel Causton, Joan Bron, Elizabeth Arundel, Margaret Burn-
  ham, Joan Spenser, Maud Pentre.
Chaplains paying 2s each: John Habraham, Thomas Lonnesdale.
Total £1 7s 4d.

7. HOSPITAL OF St BARTHOLOMEW SMITHFIELD. Prior [sic Richard Sutton]
estimated at £133 6s 8d, paying £1 10s.
Brothers paying 1s 8d each: Richard de Orewell, William de Wakeryng,
  Thomas Lakenham.
Chaplains paying 2s each: John Lyverpole, Thomas Exale.
Sisters paying 1s 8d each: Joan Pertynhale, Cecily Albon, Beatrice Squier.
Total £2 4s.

8. HOSPITAL OF St THOMAS OF ACON (Acrys in Chepe). Master estimated at
£66 13s 4d, paying £1.
Brothers paying 1s 8d each: Laurence Barnet, Richard Sewell, Thomas
  Ragdale, Nicholas Lychfeld, John Porter, Thomas Isaac.
Chaplains paying 2s each: William Edyngton, William Coupere, Richard
  Wymark, Adam Taverner, Thomas de Kent, Thomas chaplain of the
  fraternity of St John the Baptist, Thomas Fullere.
Clerk paying 4d: Richard.
Total £2 4s 4d.

9. HOSPITAL OF St ANTHONY. Master estimated at £20, paying 10s.
Chaplains paying 2s each: Thomas de Camryngham, John Coly, Thomas de
  Bekynsfeld.
Total 16s.

10. HOSPITAL OF ELSING SPITAL (St Mary de Elsyngspytle). Prior [Robert
Draycote] estimated at £66 13s 4d, paying £1.
Canons[1] paying 1s 8d each: Adam de Kent, [m. 3] Nicholas Waltham,
  Thomas Burnham, John Sonnyng, John Lovekyn.

Chaplains paying 2s each: Richard Provendre, Geoffrey Heyward, Geoffrey Rowesham.
Clerk paying 4d: William Haselee.
Total £1 14s 8d.

1. Described in the list as brothers.

11. BETHLEHEM HOSPITAL (Bedleem without Bychopgate). Master [William Titte] estimated at £10, paying 5[s].
Chaplains paying 2s each: Bro. Thomas Blakesale; John Longeford, John Dunmowe.
Total 11s.

12. CHARTERHOUSE (next Smethfeld). Prior [John Luscote] estimated at £66 13s 4d, paying £1.
Monks and brothers paying 1s 8d each: Gwydo de Burgo, Robert Hevenyngton, John Neherbury, Hugh Glowcetre, John Gryslee, Richard Halet, John Rothewell, Walter Knollys, Robert Coventre, Edmund Ballyng; Bros. Peter Mannyng, Peter Diomede (?), Thomas Rous.
Total £2 1s 8d.

13. ST MARY GRACES (next the Tower). Abbot [William de Warden] estimated at £100, paying £1 10s.
Monks paying 1s 8d each: John de Forda subprior, Thomas de Ledys, Nicholas Drayton, Jordan de Reklyswade, Semanus Passeneye, Roger subprior, Thomas de Dene.
Total £2 1s 8d.

14. CLERKENWELL (Clerkynwell). Prioress [Katherine Braybrooke] estimated at £66 13s 4d, paying £1.
Nuns paying 1s 8d each: Joan subprioress Durys, Idonia Lyter, Lucy atte Wode, Agnes Spencer, Katherine Assheford, Margaret Hawynsard, Joan Dynby, Joan Newna[m], Alice Hylleford, Beatrice Ingelard, Margaret Bacwell, Joan Vyan, Margaret Loryng, Margaret Crane, Katherine Crane, Isabel Swete.
Chaplains paying 2s each: John Baret, Richard conventual chaplain, Philip Roche, Philip Herry, John Michel.
Total £2 16s 8d.

15. MINORESSES WITHOUT ALDGATE. Abbess estimated at £100, paying £1 10s.
Sisters paying 1s 8d each: Agnes Dunbarre, Isabel Somersam, Joan Whafham, Joan Botlee, Alice Passoure, Joan Wefi, Hydda [blank], Agnes Botelor, Katherine Bewer, Margaret Waunesey, Margaret Nottelee, Joan Seynet, Alice Cros, Isabel Somersam, [m. 4] Elizabeth Ferrers, Elizabeth Darcy, Maud de Esey, Katherine Hale, Mary de Lyle, Agnes Sudbury, Sybil Maler, Margaret Holmystede, Alice Blakdene, Joan Blake, Margaret Causton, Katherine Leye.
Total £3 13s 4d.

16. St Martin le Grand. Dean [Mr Walter Skirlawe] estimated at £333 6s 8d, paying £3; pays by royal writ.
Canons.

Mr William Salusbery prebendary of [illegible] estimated at £20, paying 10s.

Mr William Mulso prebendary of [illegible] estimated at £12, paying 5s.

Mr John Skyrlowe prebendary of Faucons (Fawconers) estimated at £12, paying 5s.

John Mulso prebendary of Norton estimated at £13, paying 5s.

Mr Richard Thurban prebendary of La Coupe estimated at £5, paying 2s.

Thomas Cook prebendary of Bolbrys estimated at £10, paying 5s.

Mr Reginald Hylton prebendary of Passelewe estimated at £10, paying 5s.

William Stodley prebendary of Good Easter (Godestre) estimated at £13 6s 8d, paying 5s.

John Bawde residentiary estimated at £10, paying 5s.

Robert Morton residentiary estimated at £10, paying 5s.

Thomas Sirete (?) prebendary in Maldon (in Maldona) estimated at £10, paying 5s.

Mr Edmund Strete prebendary of Tolleshunt (Toleshonte) estimated at £4, paying 2s.

Vicars paying 2s each: John Ravenyston, Henry Clere, John Ledbury, Thomas Golde, William Lorkyn, John Staunton, William Bercamstede, Robert Fayrford, Walter Forst, Robert Hay, Walter Fayrford, John Madour, Robert Fylle.

Clerks paying 4d each: John Aghton, Philip Cowpere, John Berchamstede, Robert Sadeler.

Total £[4] 6s 4d.

17. [College of] St Lawrence Pountney (in Candylwykstret). Master [Robert Witherdeley or Wytley] estimated at £40, paying 13s 4d.

Chaplains paying 2s each: John de Northwych, Alan de Gedyngton, John Wyllyngton, Roger Grene, Walter Horewod, William Carpe, Henry Lovikyn (?), John Norhamton.

Clerk paying 4d: John.
Total £1 9s 8d.

[In **18–117** chaplains pay 2s and clerks 4d unless otherwise stated.]

18. St Andrew Holborn (Holborne). Rector estimated at £10, paying 5s.

Chaplains: Richard parochial chaplain, Roger Aldewych, John Swyneshed, Walter Whelere, Philip Bron, William Herdy, Richard chaplain of Roger Legat, William chaplain of the same Roger Legat, William Demeyn.

Clerk: John Hendone.
Total £1 3s 4d.

19. St Andrew by the Wardrobe (Beynardcastel). Rector [Richard Holmes] estimated at £10, paying 5s.

4

Chaplains: Philip Whyt, Roger Hamond, Peter Burton.
Clerk: Nicholas atte Brugge.
Total 11s 4d.

20. ST ANTONIN. Rector [John Duffeld] estimated at £20, paying 10s.
Chaplains: William Newerk, John Wermyngton, Robert Carlel, [m. 5]
Thomas Leek, John Launde, William Graunge, Thomas Gaytryng, John
Cok, Nicholas Myller(?), Thomas Colston, William chaplain of Richard
Hatfeld, Richard Sterlyng.
Clerk: John.
Total £1 14s 4d.

21. ST AUGUSTINE WATLING STREET (at the Gate). Rector [Thomas de
Kendale] estimated at £10, paying 5s.
Chaplains: Richard Pleyfeyre, William Palmer.
Clerk: John de Hyldyrston.
Total 9s 4d.

22. ST ALPHAGE LONDON WALL (Alphege). Rector [John Hall] estimated at
£10, paying 5s.
Chaplains: John Wyk, John Scheryngton.
Clerk: Robert.
Total 9s 4d.

23. ST AUDOEN. Rector has scarcely enough to live on, paying 2s.
Chaplain: John Hervy.
Total 4s.

24. ST ALBAN WOOD STREET. Rector [Richard Oudeby] estimated at £10,
paying 5s.
Chaplains: John Pynnore, William Grene, David Enyas.
Total 11s.

25. ST ETHELBURGA BISHOPSGATE. Rector [John Berford] has scarcely
enough to live on, paying 2s.
Total as above.

26. ST ANNE AND ST AGNES. Rector has scarcely enough to live on, paying
2s.
Chaplain: Peter de Venysia.
Total 4s.

27. ST ANDREW UNDERSHAFT (Cornhill). Rector estimated at £10, paying
5s.
Chaplains: John Rydere, Peter de Lynne, William Coved.
Clerks: William Colton, Thomas subclerk.
Total 11s 8d.

28. St Andrew Hubbard (Huberd). Rector estimated at £6 13s 4d, paying 2s.
Chaplain: Robert Hampschyr.
Total 4s.

29. St Augustine on the Wall (Pappey). Rector [Adam Long] has scarcely enough to live on, paying 2s.
Total as above.

30. St Botolph Bishopsgate (Botulph without Bischopgate). Rector estimated at £10, paying 5s.
Total as above.

31. St Botolph Billingsgate (Byllyngesgate). Rector estimated at £10, paying 5s.
Chaplains: John Wyttoneye, Richard Burlee, John Menel, William Stok-kyng, John Belwod, William Chaumbyrleyn, John Newhey.
Clerks: Simon Horstede, John subclerk.
Total 19s 8d.

32. St Botolph Aldgate (without Algate).
Chaplains: parochial chaplain, John chaplain of Anne Greylond.
Clerk: John.
Total 4s 4d.

33. St Botolph Aldersgate (Botulph without Aldrychgate). Rector [Ralph de Kesteven] estimated at £10, paying 5s.
Chaplains: Richard Bokysworthe, John Fulnethby, John Lytlee, Thomas matins-priest (presbyter matutinal), Richard Stanwey, John Newton, John Glazyere, William Cherchehull.
Clerk: William Est'.
Total £1 1s 4d.

34. St Benet Paul's Wharf (Powlyswharf). Rector [Richard de Everdone] estimated at £10, paying 5s.
Chaplains: Robert Molde, William Naylyston, John Tamworth, Robert Newton.
Clerk: John Corbryght.
Total 13s 4d.

35. St Benet Gracechurch (Grascherch). Rector estimated at £6 13s 4d, paying 2s.
Chaplains: Roger Rydere, [m. 6] Robert Whyt, Henry Howton, Robert Fressleford, John Andrew, Thomas Damary, Thomas Warmyngton, John Randolf.
Clerk: William Schypley subclerk.
Total 18s 4d.

36. St Benet Fink (Fynk). Rector estimated at £6 13s 4d, paying 2s.
Chaplains: William Brykhulle, William Whelplee.
Total 6s.

37. St Benet Sherehog (Schorhogg). Rector [Richard son of Vincent of Waltham Cross] estimated at £6 13s 4d, paying 2s.
Chaplains: John Michel, Adam Wynterton.
Clerk: John.
Total 6s 4d.

38. St Bartholomew by the Exchange (the Less). Rector estimated at £6 13s 4d, paying 2s.
Chaplain: Thomas Felawe.
Clerk: Thomas superior clerk.
Total 4s 4d.

39. St Bride Fleet Street (St Brigid). Rector [Thomas de Hayton] estimated at £30, paying 10s.
Chaplains: John Warde, John Lorkyn, John Brydsale, Thomas Copland, Ralph Archer, John Myddylton, John Gunthorp, John Stacbolle, John Stacbolle chaplain of Geoffrey Fourbour, John Pertynhale, Peter Grace, Walter Rysk de Irland, Richard de Wormebrygge, John chaplain of William Fourbour.
Clerk: John Stanyng.
Total £1 18s 4d.

40. Chapel of St Thomas the Martyr on the Bridge.
Chaplains: John Traylee, William Cranewell, John Whyt, William Bermyngton, William Wykyng, John Coggesale.
Total 12s.

41. St Clement Eastcheap (Eatchep). Rector [Adam Chippenham estimated at £10, paying 5s.
Chaplains: William Huchepoun, John Newton.
Total 9s.

42. St Dunstan in the West. Rector [John de Brampton] estimated at £20, paying 10s.
Chaplains: Stephen Perys, Robert Howton, John Fawn notary paying 3s 4d, John Rosse, John Umprey, John Wylton.
Total £1 3s 4d.

43. St Edmund King and Martyr (Grascherche). Rector estimated at £10, paying 5s.
Chaplains: William Belgrave, John Strauston.
Clerks: Hugh Neel, John Melborne.
Total 9s 8d.

44. St Gregory. Rector estimated at £10, paying 5s.
Chaplains: John Trygg, John Albon notary paying 3s 4d, David Lambe.
Clerk: Richard Norhampton subclerk.
Total 12s 8d.

45. St George Botolph Lane. Rector estimated at £6 13s 4d, paying 2s.
Chaplains: Richard Madour, John Benet, Geoffrey David, John Lameth,
John Baudry, Richard chaplain of the fraternity of St George.
Total 13s.

46. St John Zachary (Zakarie). Rector [Henry de Spondon] estimated at
£6 13s 4d, paying 2s.
Chaplain: Laurence Kertyl.
Total 4s.

47. St James Garlickhithe (Garlykhythe). Rector estimated at £10,
paying 5s.
Chaplains: John Wodeford, William Wylton, John Somerwell, Roger
Hunte, John Jay, John Barow, William Lude.
Total 19s.

48. St John Walbrook (in Walbrok). Rector [Thomas Pateshull] estimated
at £10, paying 5s.
Chaplains: John Wyldgos, Robert Symond.
Clerks: Richard, William.
Total 9s 8d.

49. St Katherine Coleman (Colmancherch). Rector [James Phehw]
estimated at £6 13s 4d, paying 2s.
Total as above.

50. [m. 7] St Katherine Cree (Trinity).
Chaplains: Hugh chaplain of William Creswyk, Robert Denton, Robert
Ponyngg, William Richman, Thomas Haykton, William chaplain of lady
de Hevenyngham.
Total 12s.

51. St Leonard Foster Lane (in the venell of St Vedast). Rector [Walter
Fairford] has scarcely enough to live on, paying 2s.
Chaplains: John Cambrygg, Robert Bryght.
Total 6s.

52. St Lawrence Jewry (in Iudaesino). Vicar [Robert Lepere] estimated
at £5, paying 2s.[1]
Chaplains: John Bowe, Richard Everdone, John Cyrcestre, William
Whyton, John atte Wode, Thomas Bowe, Hugh Tamworth, Philip
Russe, Richard Clerk, Thomas Tewkysbury, John Nasyngg, Richard

Hambyldon, Thomas Potynham, Henry Forde, Peter Geveyne, William Tutbury.
Clerk: William.

1. Margin: *Quare non Ritorn'*. Total at end of **53**.

53. THE GUILDHALL WITHIN THIS PARISH.
Chaplains: Mr Thomas Gravelee, William Brampton, Walter Penbrok, Peter Wysebech, John Bromleye, Edmund Noyes.
Total £2 6s 4d.

54. ST LEONARD SHOREDITCH (Schordych). Vicar estimated at £6 13s 4d, paying 2s.
Total: as above.

55. ST MICHAEL LE QUERNE (ad Bladinum). Rector [Roger Fryseby] estimated at £10, paying 5s.
Chaplains: John Dyssh, Roger Furnews, William Goldsmyth, John Wyrcestr', John Doncastr', Richard Chestr', John Brydport.
Clerk: John.
Total 19s 4d.

56. ST MICHAEL QUEENHITHE (Ripam Regine). Rector estimated at £10, paying 5s.
Chaplains: Richard Ellysworth, William Cowesby, Henry Houd, William Mody, John Budde, Walter Herford.
Clerk: Thomas.
Total 17s 4d.

57. ST MICHAEL WOOD STREET (Wodestret). Rector [John Ive or Yne] estimated at £10, paying 5s.
Chaplains: John Ledrede, Robert Brysty, William Aleyn, Robert Strekynton, John Hawkyn, William Wydlok, Adam de Reynham.
Total 19s.

58. ST MICHAEL BASSISHAW (in Bassynghawe). Rector estimated at £10, paying 5s.
Chaplains: Walter Spencer, John Pychard, Thomas Wyght, Thomas Ferrynig, William Cowlee.
Clerk: William.
Total 15s 4d.

59. ST MICHAEL CORNHILL (on Cornhell). Rector [Richard Felde] estimated at £20, paying 10s.
Chaplains: John Radenore, Hugh Tracy, Ralph Kyrkestede, William Newbald, Robert de Hedone, Thomas de Burton, Simon Baret, William Boreford, [m. 8] William Bocklee, William Aylston.
Total £1 10s.

60. St Mary Aldermanbury (Aldyrmanbury). Rectory is appropriated to the hospital of Elsing Spital.
Chaplains: Reginald atte Halle, Nicholas de Vundlee, Nicholas Smothe.
Clerk: John.
Chaplain: William Furnews.
Total 8s 4d.

61. St Mary Woolnoth (Wolnoth). Rector estimated at £6 13s 4d, paying 2s.
Chaplain: John Peienne.
Clerk: Roger.
Total 4s 4d.

62. St Mary Axe (atte Ax). Rector has scarcely enough to live on, paying 2s.
Total as above.

63. St Mary Abchurch (Abchyrch). Rector estimated at £10, paying 5s.
Chaplains: Thomas Snoryng, John Burham, Robert Asshewell, William Woleaston.
Clerks: William superior clerk, John inferior clerk.
Total 13s 8d.

64. St Mary Woolchurch (Wolcherchawe). Rector [John Dyne] estimated at £10, paying 5s.
Chaplains: John Malton, Thomas Browghton, John Seley, Thomas Brymmysgrove, John Myldrede.
Clerk: John Wodeham.
Total 15s 4d.

65. St Mary Somerset (Somerete). Rector [Simon Tuk or Tukke] estimated at £10, paying 5s.
Chaplain: Thomas Capon.
Clerk: John.
Total 7s 4d.

66. St Mary Mounthaw (Mountenhuc). Rector has scarcely enough to live on, paying 2s.
Chaplains: Stephen Walsche, Stephen Walsyngham.
Total 6s.

67. St Mary Staining (Stanynglane). Rector has scarcely enough to live on, paying 2s.
Total as above.

68. St Mary Colechurch (Colcherch). Rectory is appropriated to the college [sic] of St Thomas of Acon (Acres).
Chaplains: John Northfolk, Henry Taylour, John Smelt, Bartholomew Nyne, John Turnour, John Dorslee, John Spencer.

Clerk: Thomas.
Total 14s 4d.

69. St Mary at Hill (atte Hull). Rector [Adam Berden] estimated at £10, paying 5s.
Chaplains: John Housebond, William Belde, William Stepworth.
Clerk: John Andrew.
Total 11s 4d.

70. St Gabriel Fenchurch (St Mary Fancherch). Rector [John Hontoft or Honcroft] estimated at £6 13s 4d, paying 2s.
Chaplain: John Gerford.
Clerk: John Halyngbury.
Total 4s 4d.

71. St Mary Islington (Isyldone). Vicar estimated at £5, paying 2s.
Chaplain: John Wyte.
Total 4s.

72. St Mary Magdalen Milk Street (Melkstreet). Rector [William de Somerdaby] estimated at £10, paying 5s.
Chaplains: William Salman, Andrew Renel, John Schypthorp, John Wermyngton, John Phylyp, Nicholas Aubel.
Clerks: John Bedeford superior clerk, John Stondone inferior clerk.
[m. 9] Total 17s 8d.

73. St Mary Magdalen Old Fish Street (in Veteri Pisc'). Rector estimated at £10, paying 5s.
Chaplains: William Northwych, Philip Rauton, Roger Skrafeld.
Clerk: John.
Chaplain: John Stouhard.
Total 13s 4d.

74. St Margaret Fish Street Hill (at the Bridge). Rector [Robert Sprotborough] estimated at £10, paying 5s.
Chaplains: William de Kenyan, John de Bevyrley.
Total 9s.

75. St Margaret Lothbury. Rector [Roger de Faringdon] estimated at £6 13s 4d, paying 2s.
Chaplains: William de Warmyngton, Richard Smeth, William Noyer, William Ammory, Gilbert Betrych.
Clerk: William Salman superior clerk, William Pelgrene inferior clerk.
Total 12s 8d.

76. St Margaret Pattens (Patenys). Rector [John Stakbole] has scarcely enough to live on, paying 2s.
Chaplains: Elias Archer, Thomas chaplain of John atte Vyne draper.
Clerk: John.
Total 6s 4d.

77. St Margaret Moses Friday Street (Moysy). Rector [Geoffrey le Spencer] estimated at £10, paying 5s.
Chaplains: John chaplain of John Aquitayne, William Goldryng.
Clerk: Robert.
Total 9s 4d.

78. St Mildred Poultry (in Pultria). Rector estimated at £10, paying 5s.
Chaplains: John Carwyle, Richard Wyk, Robert Marchal.
Clerk: John Ketyn.
Total 11s 4d.

79. St Mildred Bread Street (in Bredstret). Rector [William Godrigg] estimated at £6 13s 4d, paying 2s.
Chaplains: John Tolworth, John Tykhull, Richard Coonen, John Wysebech, John Bynbrok, John Stormysworth, John Betewyk.
Clerk: Stephen.
Total 16s 4d.

80. St Martin Orgar. Rector estimated at £10, paying 5s.
Chaplains: Richard Mahomid, Nicholas Curteys, Robert Whythod, Nicholas Swaffham, John Watkyn, John Heyworth.
Clerk: Thomas.
Total 17s 4d.

81. St Martin Ludgate. Rector estimated at £20, paying 10s.
Chaplains: Roger Schereve, Robert Clerk, Simon Symond, William Staunston, William Blakburne, John Mulsham, John Bywell, William Chestane.
Clerk: Thomas Page.
Total £1 6s 4d.

82. St Martin Vintry (in Vinteria). Rector [Roger Dunster or Halfree] estimated at £10, paying 5s.
Chaplains: John Howton, John Forster, Robert Stylere, Thomas Bertlot, Richard dwelling with Cornwaleys.
Total 15s.

83. St Martin Pomery (de Pomerio). Rector estimated at £6 13s 4d, paying 2s.
Chaplains: Thomas Barwe, Richard Frend, John Gylot, Stephen Benet.
Clerk: Walter.
Total 10s 4d.

84. St Martin Oteswich (Oteswych). Rector [William de Paxton] estimated at £6 13s 4d, paying 2s.
Chaplain: Walter Walsche.
Total 4s.

85. St Matthew Friday Street (in Frydaystret). Rector estimated at £10, paying 5s.
Chaplains: John Weston, William Melbourne, John Reygate.
Clerks: Robert Haunsy, Thomas.
Total 11s 8d.

86. St Magnus the Martyr. Rector [Walter Browne] estimated at £30, paying 10s.
Chaplains: John Stanston, Robert Westby, John Notyngham, Nicholas Campdene, John Cantyrbury, Thomas Bampton, Robert Walsokene, Lambert Seland, John Lyndeseye, [m. 10] John de Burdews, Philip Canaan.
Clerk: William subclerk.
Total £1 12s 4d.

87. St Nicholas Shambles (ad Macellum). Rector estimated at £20, paying 10s.
Chaplains: Robert Langlee, John Malton, Thomas Hampthylle, William Ingylby, Ralph Overton, Thomas Wysebach.
Clerk: John Plymer.
Total £1 2s 4d.

88. St Nicholas Cole Abbey (Coldabbey). Rector [John Baud] estimated at £10, paying 5s.
Chaplains: William Bacwell, William Jowel, John Notton, Ralph Bonyngton, John Borham, John Hyndcley, John Therborw, Robert de Eton, John de Rufton, Robert de Tryntham, Thomas de Inkflete.
Clerk: John Stebynhythe.
Total £1 7s 4d.

89. St Nicholas Acon. Rector [William Bennington] estimated at £6 13s 4d, paying 2s.
Chaplain: John Hawkyn.
Total 4s.

90. St Nicholas Olave (Olof). Rector [Henry de Welewes] has scarcely enough to live on, paying 2s.
Chaplains: Thomas Palmer, Adam Duure de Herford, Nicholas Blyseworthe, John de Ratforde.
Total 10s.

91. All Hallows Barking (Omnium Sanctorum Berkyng). Rector [Thomas de Dalby] estimated at £20, paying 10s.
Chaplains: Richard Grettone, John Cornewayle, Adam Baldewene, John Rood.
Total 18s.

92. All Hallows Honey Lane (Omnium Sanctorum Honeylane). Rector estimated at £10, paying 5s.

13

Chaplains: Robert Longeman, Thomas Schertegrave, Nicholas Leche, William Mewt.
Clerk: John Downys.
Total 13s 4d.

93. ALL HALLOWS THE GREAT (Omnium Sanctorum ad Fenum). Rector estimated at £10, paying 5s.
Chaplains: John Warewyk, William de Coventr', Adam de Sowthmarton, William de Herford, John Veel, Walter Yerdelee.
Clerk: Nicholas.
Total 17s 4d.

94. ALL HALLOWS THE LESS (Omnium Sanctorum super Celarium). Rectory is appropriated to the college of St Lawrence Pountney (Pontneye).
Chaplains: Richard Bylermyng (?), Reginald chaplain of Edmund Oliver, Roger chaplain of James Andrew.
Total 6s.

95. ALL HALLOWS STAINING (Omnium Sanctorum Stanyngcherch). Rectory is appropriated to the abbey of St Mary Graces.
Chaplains: John Haylys, John Kent, William Walsche, Eustace Sunday, John Appeweyn.
Clerks: Robert superior clerk, Henry inferior clerk.
Total 10s 8d.

96. ST OLAVE OLD JEWRY (in Judaisino). Rectory is appropriated to the abbey of [blank].
Chaplains: Adam Brekespere, William Baye.
Clerk: Thomas Geddyngg.
Total 4s 4d.

97. ST OLAVE HART STREET (by the Tower). Rector [William de Gildes-burgh] estimated at £10, paying 5s.
Chaplains: Thomas Besewyk, Ralph Blythe.
Total 9s.

98. ST OLAVE SILVER STREET (Mugwell). Rector estimated at £6 13s 4d, paying 2s.
Chaplain: Robert Layghton.
Total 4s.

99. [m. 11] ALL HALLOWS LONDON WALL (at the Wall). Rector estimated at £6 13s 4d, paying 2s.
Chaplain: William Senesterrys.
Total 4s.

100. ST PETER LE POOR (Bradstret). Rector [Henry Bever] has scarcely enough to live on, paying 2s.
Chaplain: John Barton.
Total 4s.

101. ST PETER PAUL'S WHARF (the Less). Rector [Robert de Kyrkeby] estimated at £6 13s 4d, paying 2s.
Chaplains: Simon Marchal, David Penne, John David.
Total 8s.

102. ST PETER CORNHILL (Cornhell). Rector [John Mansyn] estimated at £10, paying 5s.
Chaplains: Peter de Fledborwgh, John de Norwold, John Heyward, John de Lewe, Roger chaplain of lady de Nevyle.
Clerk: John Trowyn.
Total 15s 4d.

103. ST PETER WESTCHEAP (in Chepe). Rector [John Joye] estimated at £10, paying 5s.
Chaplains: John Whynne, Simon de Brennysgrave, Richard Fulham, Walter Selam, Nicholas Hauley, John Fysch, John Huet.
Clerk: Peter Byk'.
Total 19s 4d.

104. ST STEPHEN WALBROOK (Walbrok). Rector [Robert Ellerker or de Alderker] estimated at £20, paying 10s.
Chaplains: John Spark, Ralph Aldrystone, John Treygoph', William chaplain of Adam de Bury, Robert Chadworth, John Irysch.
Clerks: John Aston superior clerk, John inferior clerk.
Total £1 2s 8d.

105. ST STEPHEN COLEMAN STREET (Colmanstret). Rectory is appropriated to the prior of Butley (Botlee).
Chaplains: John vicar of the church, John Elmyswell, John Botlee, John Eyton, John Sexel, Roger Hornwode, Nicholas Hancherch.
Total 14s.

106. ST SWITHIN. Rector [John de Burton] estimated at £10, paying 5s.
Chaplains: Robert Cululli, Walter Capon, Richard Crosby notary (paying 3s 4d), John chaplain of Robert Rous.
Clerk: John Gardyner.
Total 14s 8d.

107. ST SEPULCHRE NEWGATE. Church is appropriated to the prior of St Bartholomew Smithfield (Smethefeld).
Chaplains: Adam Brykkysworthe vicar there, Thomas Eydone, John Eydone, John Benet, Roger Staunford, William Abyngton, John Weston, William Colyngham.
Total 16s.

108. ST THOMAS THE APOSTLE. Rector estimated at £6 13s 4d, paying 2s.
Chaplains: William Kynggyshows, John Huet, Thomas Padworthe.
Clerk: William Barker.
Total 8s 4d.

109. HOLY TRINITY THE LESS. Rector estimated at £6 13s 4d, paying 2s.
Chaplains: John Randolf, John Rok, John Boursee, John Brydport,
William Wychyngham, William Cryps, Hugh Lyntone.
Total 16s.

110. ST CHRISTOPHER (Xpopheri). Rector [Thomas de Coldyngton]
estimated at £20, paying 10s.
Chaplains: Simon Schyrland, John Kerdyngton, John Wade, John Bolee,
John Bevyrley, Thomas Hytwey, Thomas Langby, John Merdon, John
Bokyngham, [m. 12] Walter chaplain of Adam Carlel.
Clerk: John Fraunkeleyn.
Total £1 10s 4d.

111. ST GILES CRIPPLEGATE (Crepylgate). Vicar [John Trowbrigge] esti-
mated at £20, paying 10s.
Chaplains: Thomas Clerk, John Altecr', William Henry, Simon Hekpol,
John Fyraverey, William de Astone, William Helkneye, William Habra-
ham, Henry Wellyngton.
Clerks: Adam Sothewell, Robert (?) subclerk.
Total £1 8s 8d.

112. THE NEW TEMPLE. Master: Bro. John Bartylby, paying 3s 4d.
Chaplains: Robert Kyrkeby, Thomas Weston, William Eversam, Bernard
Barton.
Total 11s 4d.

113. Clerks of the chapel of lady de Norfolk (Norrfolk): John Selby,
Nicholas, Richard, Henry.
Total 1s 4d.

114. Clerks of the Official of the Archdeacon: John Bassyngborne, Robert
Brandone.
Total 8d.

115.[1] John Rosse clerk of St Olave Silver Street (Muguuell), paying 4d.
William subclerk of St Stephen Coleman Street (Colmanstrete), paying 4d.
William subclerk of St Bartholomew by the Exchange (the Less), paying 4d.
John Munc paying 2s.
William Bevorley paying 2s.
Henry Beneger notary paying 3s 4d.
Henry More celebrating in Coleman Street paying 2s.
John Stretley celebrating in the church of St Helen paying 2s.
William Stanforde celebrating at Mounthaw (Montehaut) paying 2s.
William subclerk of Bartholomew by the Exchange paying 4d.
William subclerk of St Stephen Coleman Street paying 4d.
Robert chaplain of Thomas ate Horcho paying 2s.
Total 19s.

1. New hand.

116.[1] HOSPITAL OF ST KATHERINE BY THE TOWER. Master: John de Hermesthorp, estimated at £100 for all his benefices, paying £1 10s.
Chaplains: William Bouges, Ed[ward] James, Nicholas, Thomas Gowes.
Sisters paying 1s each: Katherine, Alice Cove, Gylemotte.
   1. New hand.

117. CHAPLAINS.
Peter de Gascon celebrating at Castle Baynard (Baynardescastel).
John Chyvele celebrating at Garlickhithe (Garlikhithe).
Peter de Franc' celebrating at Staining (Stanynglane).
Herbert celebrating at Coleman Street.
Richard Dautr' celebrating in the church of St Peter Cornhill (Cornhull).
John Knolles celebrating at Barking (Berkynge) church.

Sum total received: £110 6s 4d.

SUBSIDY OF 1380 IN THE CITY OF LONDON

118. [E179/42/9 face col. 1] Names of priests and notaries in the city and archdeaconry of London each of whom pays 2s for the subsidy granted to the king in the third year [of his reign] viz:
John Umfrey chaplain, Roger chaplain of Jordan de Barton, John Little, Robert Houghton, John Foun, Andrew Waryn, Thomas Coupland, John Garthorp, John Pertenale, John Stakeboll, John Lekhampsted, John Norton, Ralph chaplain of a perpetual chantry, John Action, John Stakboll jun., John Warde, Peter Stockton, Walter Reys, Richard Bokesworth, William Dymayn.

119. John Smyth, Philip Broun, Walter Norman, Richard priest of Roger Leget, Thomas Eydon, John Beneyt, William Bate, John Staunford, John Eydon, John atte Spitele, Roger Haket, Robert Clerc, Simon celebrating for the fraternity of St John Baptist, William Kesteven, John Colfot, John Drayton, John Fulnadby, Richard Stanewey, John Neuton, Thomas chaplain.

120. Roger chaplain, John chaplain, Walter chaplain, William de Cherchehull, Thomas Felawe, Robert Brampton, William Ellerton, William Veyse, John Beverle, John Wytton, Walter Rous, William de Warmyngton, Richard Smyth, William Aumory, William Evesham, Simon de Shirland, John Morton, John Sibthorp, John Wade, Thomas Longeley, *60*.

121. John Rademere, Hugh Tracy, William Neubalt, Robert Hedon, Thomas de Boughton, Simon Baret, William Bereford, William Botteler, William chaplain, Thomas Broughton, John Sely, John Pynchebek, William Warrewyk, John Fakenham, John Hampton, Nicholas Senestre, Thomas chaplain, William Hereford, Robert chaplain, William Bren.

17

122. Adam Reynham, Richard Reynold, John Ledred, Robert Bresty, William Aleyn, Thomas Dautre, William Seustern, John Burgulon, Robert Reygate, William Furneux, Robert Hampdeby, John Arnald, William Melbourne, William Palmere, Thomas Bekenesfeld, John Wyldegoos, [col. 2] Stephen de Crepulgate, Robert Studeye, Walter Norfolk, Nicholas Derby.

123. Ralph Curteys, Thomas Lonnesdale, John Cantebrugge, Thomas Exale, Robert Bright, Peter de Fleteburgh, Henry de Peryndon, John de le Ewe, William Noir, William Tikton, John Derham, John Hayward, Peter de Thaksted, John Abraham, John Wircestre, William Teukesbury, Robert Furneux, John Disse, Laurence Kellishull, Thomas Donynton, *60*.

124. Walter Spencer, Thomas Ferthyng, William Bras, Thomas Whyte, John Pychard, John Pisford, Robert Langeley, Thomas Hampton, Hugh Sourdenale, John Malton, Thomas Snoryng, John Haykyng, John Ruston, Ralph de Donyngton, William Juell, John Wyncestre, Robert Spaldyng, John Wyrcestre, Thomas de Ynkflete, Thomas Palmere.

125. John Grewe, William chaplain, William Belgyan, John chaplain, John Langston, Henry de Shelford, John de Raundes, Walter Wilby, Stephen de Walsyngham, Robert chaplain, John de Wrestlyngford, John chaplain, John Norfolk, Bartholomew Dyne, John Turnour, John Smelt, John Dursle, Thomas Gisele, Thomas Cok, William Grifph (?).

126. William Heyham, John Albon, John Rous, William Horn, William Gausby, John Bude, John Catton, William Welles, David chaplain, William Grew, John Stalham, Reginald atte Hall, Nicholas de Vudele, Henry de Rothewell, Nicholas Norfolk, John Raudeby, William Kyngeshous, John Howet, John Essex, John Besewyk, *60*.

127. John Tykell, John Wysebech, John Stormesworth, William Forster, Thomas Besewyk, John Dumbeley, Robert Ryngwode, Thomas Bartlot, the chaplain of Cornwaleis, John Michell, Adam de Wyntirton, William de Goldre, Thomas chaplain, John Durham, David Pen, William Hokkele, Robert Brunne, Richard Foulham, Simon de Brymesgrove, Walter Selham, *100*.

128. Nicholas Haubegh, [dorse col. 1] John Whyn, John Huwet, William Blakbourne, William Tregowe, John Spark, Robert Queryngham, William Puryton, Adam Tanner, William Edyngdon, William Couper, John Dene, Thomas Kent, Thomas Wynchecombe, John Cantuar, Robert chaplain, John Notyngham, Philip chaplain, John Lyndeseye, Lambert chaplain.

129. John Staunton, Richard Everdon, John Circestre, Hugh Tampworth, Thomas Bowe, Richard Clerc, John atte Wode, Peter Gyneyve (?), Henry Ford, Geoffrey Rousham, William Tuttebury, Thomas Teukesbury, Robert Halyday, John Nasyng, Richard Hameldon, Philip Russe, John Michell, John Juyll, Richard de Dene, Robert Fresshford, *60*.

130. John White, William Kellesey, Reginald Meteford, John Lax, John Warmynton, John Newerk, Andrew chaplain, Robert Langman, William Mought, Nicholas Lecche, Thomas Shortgrave, Robert Culhull, John Southfolk, Nicholas Swafham, Adam Smyth, John Northwich, Alan Gedynton, Robert Fille, John Wylton, Richard Burstowe.

131. William Chappe, Roger atte Grene, Henry Lovenham, John de Wyllughton, Roger Hunte, Albert chaplain, John Antoyne, John Barewe, John Jay, William Lount, Thomas Bere, William Aylesdon, John Wytteneye, Richard Gurle, William Stakyng, John Menell, John Bellewode, John Elmeswell, John Pavy, John Butle.

132. Robert Gore, Roger Horewode, Herbert Fraunceys, Henry atte More, Richard chaplain, Thomas Capoun, Robert Perpount, William Richeman, Thomas Aykton, Henry Myles, John chaplain, Adam Brekespere, William Bathe, John Sexell, William Wolaston, Simon Marchall, John Wyk, Henry Poyntell, John Albon, † [sic] David Lambe, *60*.

133. Philip Whyte, Thomas Grene, Roger chaplain, John Covyntre, † six chaplains in the New Temple, † six chaplains in the Guildhall chapel, [dorse col. 2] † four chaplains in the chapel on London bridge, † eleven chaplains in St Martin's chapel, John Whityng, Walter chaplain, John chaplain, Thomas Olthorp, John Herdwyk, John Tampworth, Thomas Clerc, William chaplain, Robert Neuton, John Churchehull, John Baret, John chaplain.

134. Philip chaplain, Philip chaplain S P, Thomas chaplain, Adam chaplain, William Covyntre, Walter Lyndon, Adam chaplain, John Warrewyk, Philip chaplain, William Newerk, Robert Carlill, John Anne, William atte Corner, Thomas Gadrik, Thomas Leek, John Cook, William chaplain, John Leycestre, Richard Flore, William Lenge.

135. John Asshfeld, Thomas Barewe, Richard Frend, Stephen Benet, Richard chaplain, Robert Overton, William Abraham, Simon Ekepoll, Thomas Bateman, Henry Welenton, William chaplain, Roger chaplain, William chaplain, Richard Procurator, John Benet, Robert chaplain, Robert fraternity chaplain, Peter chaplain, William chaplain, William Walssh.

136. John Feith, Hugh Dannebury, William Norhampton, Nicholas chaplain, John Watford, John Straunge, William Stoke, John Fisshere, Nicholas Lese, Bartholomew Alman, John Huchon, Peter Grace, Thomas Peys,[1] John Kerdynton, William chaplain, *33*.

1. Not described as 'dominus'.

137. TOTAL – of priests 409[1] . 20[2]
304 . 18[2] priests and rectors
– subsidy £40 . 18s
£39 . 16s[2] viz. for each priest 2s.

1. Rectius 398.
2. Crossed through.

138. NOTARIES PUBLIC. Henry Quyng, John Lynton, paying 2s each. *Approved.* Sum total of the subsidy of priests and notaries £41 2s.
Item to the subsidy of advocates, proctors, or registrars unbeneficed and not paying the fifteenth there is no answer because none of these advocates, proctors or registrars could be found in the city or archdeaconry of London as is testified on oath.

139. [dorse col. 3] Rectors whose benefices are not assessed for payment of the subsidy because of the poverty of their benefices, viz. rector of St Augustine on the Wall (Pappay), rector of St Audoen, rector of St Anne and St Agnes, rector of St Katherine Coleman (Colman), vicar of St Laurence Jewry (in Iudaisino), rector of St Mary Axe (at Nax), rector of St Mary Mounthaw, rector of St Mary Staining (Stanyng), rector of St Nicholas Olave, rector of St Peter le Poor (in Bradstrete), vicar of St Leonard Shoreditch.

POLL TAX OF 1381 IN THE CATHEDRAL AND ITS JURISDICTION

140. [E 179/42/10 m. 1] Particulars of the account of William Coleyn canon of the cathedral church of London, collector of the subsidy granted to king Richard II by the clergy in convocation (apud parliamentum) at Northampton in the fourth year [of his reign] within the said cathedral church and the peculiar jurisdiction of its dean and chapter, viz. from the said subsidy as follows:
BENEFICED [all paying 6s 8d unless otherwise stated]
John Appelby dean, Richard Perynton archdeacon of Colchester, Roger Holm chancellor, Thomas Bakton archdeacon of London, Henry Wynterton archdeacon of Essex, Amandus Fytlyng canon, John Wade canon, William Coloyne, William Navesby, William Dyghton, Martin Elys rector of St Faith, the vicar of St Giles without Cripplegate (Crepulgate), Thomas rector of St Gregory, John vicar of Chiswick (Chesewyk), John vicar of Navestock (Navestok) *owes 2s*, William vicar of Belchamp St Paul's (Belechamp) *owes 3s 4d*.

141. [BENEFICED cont.] Thomas vicar of Wickham St Paul's (Wykham), Gregory vicar of Walton on the Naze, Robert vicar of Kirby le Soken (Kyrkeby), Walter vicar of Thorpe le Soken (Thorp'), Richard vicar of Heybridge (Heybrygg), John vicar of Tillingham (Tyllyngham), John vicar of Asheldham (Asseldham), John vicar of Barling (Barlyng), William vicar of Willesden (Wyllysdon), John vicar of West Drayton, Thomas vicar of St Pancras Middlesex (in Campo), William rector of Stoke Newington (Stokenewenton) *non sol'*, the rector of Twyford (Twyford Parva) *non sol'*, the prioress of St Helen, Martin Elys rector of St Faith, Richard vicar of Lee Chapel (Westle) 3s 4d *non sol'*.

142. UNBENEFICED. Thomas Croxton 5s 4d, William Ryffyn 5s, John Norwych 5s, John Albon 4s 2d, Robert Salle 4s 2d, Robert Norwych 3s 11½d, Robert Albotesle 3s 11½d, John Potton 4s 5d, William Wyrcestre

4s 7d, William Dayvyle 4s 8½d, Richard Houper 3s 10d, Robert Dokesworth 3s 10d.

143. [UNBENEFICED cont.] Adam Gaddesby 3s 11½d, John Halstede 3s 11¼d, Thomas Bysshop 3s 11½d, Ralph Twyford 4s, William Revel 3s 11½d, Ralph Multon 4s 2d, John Hyltoft 4s 2d, Warin Medborne 4s 4d *non sol'*, David Mort 4s 10d, Roger Feltwell 3s 11¼d, John Zatton 3s 4d, Thomas Boudon 3s 10d.

144. [UNBENEFICED cont.] [All paying 3s 4d:] John Feyth, John Watfordd, Nicholas Barbur, *60* Hugh Bannebury, William Norhampton, John chaplain of Agnes Franceys, William chaplain of the prioress, Henry Godselawe, John Cotes, the chaplain of William Tomer, John Fytzavery, Robert Querton, William Abraham, Henry Wylyndon, Henry More.

145. [UNBENEFICED cont.] Simon Ekpol, Thomas Batman, John Albon, William chaplain of William Porter *non sol'*, Richard chaplain of St Faith, William chaplain of St [sic] Amandus Fytlyng, John Amys chaplain of Wickham St Paul's, Walter chaplain of Tillingham (Tylyngham), John chaplain of Willesden (Wyllesdon), William Wolaston, William Cheston *non sol'*, John Bukworth, Margaret subprioress of St Helen, Katherine Wolf.

146. [m. 2] Names of persons in St Paul's cathedral and within the peculiar jurisdiction of the dean and chapter paying divers sums, specified below, towards the subsidy granted to the king in the fourth year of his reign by the clergy in convocation (in parliamento) at Norhampton; that is, to the help and succour of other persons of less substance. These people mentioned below are not to be reckoned among the number of other persons paying towards this subsidy.
John Appelby dean 3s 4d, Richard Perynton archdeacon of Colchester 3s 4d, Roger Holm chancellor 3s 4d, Thomas Bakton archdeacon of London 3s 4d, Henry Wynterton archdeacon of Middlesex [recte Essex] 3s 4d, Amandus Fytlyng canon 3s, John Wade canon 1s 8d, William Coloyne 1s 10d, William Navesby 1s, William Dyghton 5s 4d, William Pakynton 1s 8d, William Fulborne 6s 8d.

147. Henry Snayth 2s 8d, William Terynton 1s 8d, William Wenlok 1s 10d, William Chesulden 2s 4d, William Shrovesbury 1s, John Wendlyngburgh 3s, Thomas Aston 1s 3d, John Dysford 1s, Thomas Crocer 1s 8d, Robert Bradgar 1s 4d, John Swynle 2s 8d, William Gotham 2s 6d.

148. John Berkyng 1s 6d, John Donewych 2s 2½d, Adam Wygmore 1s, William Oxwyk 2s 4d, Thomas Strete 1s 1d, Simon Steynton 1s 7d, Adam Damport 2s 6d, John Maundur 4s 11d *non sol'*, William Rodris 3s 4d, Martin Elys 3s 8d, John Purle 4s, John Croxton 2s 4d.

149. Richard Pertenhale 3s 4d, Bartholomew Attelburgh 2s 6d, Richard Cotel 2s 6d, John Lynton 2s 8d, John Cristemasse 2s 4d, Richard Everdon 6d, Henry Welwes 7½d, Robert Kyrkeby 6d, John Redhod 6d, Reginald Spaldyng 8d, William Brydbrok 7½d, Nicholas Wasshyngborn 7½d.

150. William Copmanthorp 1s, John Brewode 1s, Adam Prytewell 3d, Philip Keys 5d, William Barton 8d, William Salman 3d, Thomas Kendale 7½d, John Pencrych 6d, Robert Franceis 6d, John Combe 3d, John Bukworth 2d, Henry Bever 6d.

151. John Trobbrygg 5s, the rector of St Gregory 5s, John vicar of Chiswick 2s, John Gromond vicar of Navestock 2s 6d, William vicar of Belchamp St Paul's 5s, Thomas vicar of Wickham St Paul's 3s 4d, Gregory vicar of Walton on the Naze 3s 4d, Robert vicar of Kirby le Soken 3s 4d, Walter vicar of Thorpe le Soken 3s 4d, Richard vicar of Heybridge 3s 4d, John vicar of Tillingham 5s, John vicar of Asheldham 1s.

152. John vicar of Barling 2s 6d, William vicar of Willesden 2s 8d, John vicar of West Drayton 2s 6d, Thomas vicar of St Pancras Middlesex 3s 4d, William vicar of Stoke Newington 3s 4d, the prioress of St Helen, London £3 *non sol'*.

153. Approved. Total: £11 11s 2½d.
[Illegible. Sum total?] of other receipts: £36 9s 3½d.
[Illegible.]   £1 2s 7½d.
Sum total of receipts: £37 3s 3½d.

154. [m. 3] Names of persons from whom William Coleyn, canon of London cathedral, collector of the subsidy granted to the king by the clergy at Northampton in the fourth year of king Richard II within the said cathedral and the peculiar jurisdiction of its dean and chapter, levies nothing to the king's use because those persons pay elsewhere in the dioceses specified below.
City of London.[1]
Henry Welwes, St Nicholas Olave (Olouf); Richard Everdon, St Benet Paul's Wharf (Pouleswharf); Robert Kyrkeby, St Peter Paul's Wharf (Parvi Pouleswharf); John Redhod, St Martin Pomery; Reginald Spaldyng, St Benet Gracechurch (Greschyrch); Thomas Kendale, St Augustine Watling Street; John Coumbe, St Nicholas Shambles (ad Mascellas); William Morn, St Michael Queenhithe; Henry Bever, St Peter le Poor.
The prior of Elsing Spital and the rector of St Nicholas Cole Abbey, London, collectors in the city answer for these items in their account.

1. The material on this membrane is arranged in three columns. In the left hand margin is shown the area of jurisdiction within which the benefice lies; in the centre are the incumbents and their benefices, the entries here being literally translateable as 'Concerning dominus AB there is no answer because he pays at his church of St C'; the right hand column shows the collector or collectors in that area.

155. *Jurisdiction of Canterbury.*
Adam Prytewell, All Hallows Lombard Street (Greschirch).
The same Adam and Robert de Bere collectors in the deanery of Bow (Arches) answer for this item in their account.
Answers. William Barton, St Olave Silver Street (Mogwell): 6s 8d.

156. *Archdeaconry of Essex.*
William Copmanthorp, Ingatestone (Gyng ad Petram), Chelmsford (Chelmesford) deanery; William Wendlyngburgh, Theydon Garnon (Thedon Gernon), Ongar (Angre) deanery; Nicholas Wasshyngborn, Laver Magdalen (Lauvar Maudeleyn), Ongar deanery; John Purle, Purleigh (Purle), Dengie (Dansey) deanery.
The abbot of [St Mary] Graces, London and the prior of Leighs (Lewes) collectors answer for these items.
Archdeaconry of Middlesex.
Philip Cavel, vicarage of Bishop's Stortford (Storteford), in the archdeaconry of Middlesex, Braughing (Braghyng) deanery.
The prior of Holy Trinity, London, collector, answers for this item.
Archdeaconry of Essex.
William Lyndon, Little Warley (Warle Parva).
The abbot of [St Mary] Graces and the prior [of Leighs] answer for this item.

157. *Hertford. Lincoln diocese.*[1]
William Brydbrok, Welwyn (Welwes).
The prior of Newnham (Newenham) collector answers for this item.
    1. 'Lincoln diocese' after an omission sign.

158. *Archdeaconry of Middlesex.*
Richard Pertenale, Acton, in Middlesex deanery.
The prior of Holy Trinity collector answers for this item.
Answers. Lincoln diocese.
Richard Cotal, Barnet: 6s 8d.

159. *Lincoln diocese. Archdeaconries of Huntingdon and Bedford (Bedeford).*
Thomas Aston, Warboys (Wardeboys), St Ives deanery; John Swynle archdeacon of Huntingdon, Huntingdon deanery; William Wenlok, Woodhil (Wodhulle), Clapham (Clopham) deanery; John Dyfford, Watton, Hertford (Hertfordd) deanery.
The prior of Newnham collector answers for these items.
Archdeaconries of Oxford (Oxon') and Buckingham.
Thomas Strete, Haseley (Hasle); William Pakynton, Ivinghoe (Yvyngho), Mursley (Muresle) deanery.
The abbot of Notley (Nottele) collector answers for these items.
Archdeaconry of Northampton.
The rector of Thrapston, Oundle (Oundele) deanery.
Archdeaconry of Leicester.
Nicholas Sekyndon, Markfield (Merkfeld), Sparkenhoe (Sperkenhowe) deanery.
The prior of Daventry collector answers for these items.

160. *Archdeaconry of Middlesex.*
John Donewych, Barley (Barle), Braughing deanery.
The prior of Holy Trinity, London, collector answers for this item.

161. *Lincoln diocese.*
William Chesuldon, Titchmarsh (Tychemersh).
The prior of Daventry collector answers for this item.
John Brewode, King's Ripton (Kyngesrypton); William Salman, Shenley
(Shonele).
The prior of Newnham collector answers for these items.
Newport (*Neuport*) *deanery.*
William Sutton, Stoke Hammond (Stokhamund).
The abbot of Notley answers for this item.

162. *Ely diocese.*
Henry Snayth, Haddenham (Hadenham), Ely deanery; John Croxton,
Croxton, Bourn (Brunne) deanery.
Abbot of Thorney collector answers for these items.
Answers. William Fulburne, Fulbourn (Fulburne): 6s 8d.

163. *Archdeaconries of Norwich and Norfolk.*
William rector of Shipdham (Shypdam), Hingham (Hengham) deanery;
John rector of Diss (Dysshe), Redenhall (Redenhale) deanery; Adam
rector of Hockwold (Hokeweld), Cranwich (Carnewyz) deanery; Adam
rector of St Peter Hungate (Hundgate), Norwich deanery.
The prior of Walsingham (Walsyngham) collector answers for these items.
William rector of Hartest (Herthurst), archdeaconry of Sudbury.
The priors of Butley and St Peter Ipswich (Gippewici) collectors answer for
this item.

164. *Archdeaconry of Worcester.*
Philip rector of Budbrooke (Budbrok), Warwick (Warrewych) deanery.
The prior of Worcester cathedral collector answers for this item.
Answers. Robert Fraunceys, Clopton (Copham): 6s 8d.

165. *Archdeaconry of Canterbury.*
Robert rector of Hollingbourne (Holyngburne), Sutton deanery.
The prior of St Gregory, Canterbury collector answers for this item.
Jurisdiction of Canterbury.
Rector of St Mary Bothaw (Buthehawe); John rector of St Vedast (Vadast).
In the deanery of St Mary le Bow. Robert Bere and Adam Prytewell collec-
tors answer for these items.

166. *Archdeaconry of Chichester.*
William rector of Petworth (Petteworth), Midhurst deanery.
The prior of Tortington (Tortyngton) collector answers for this item.

167. *Rochester diocese.*
Rector of North Cray (Northcreye), Dartford (Dertford) deanery.
The prior of Rochester cathedral collector answers for this item.

168. *Bath* [*and Wells*] *diocese.*
Simon Steynton,[1] Brympton, Yeovil (Yevele) deanery.

The prior of Taunton collector answers for this item.
   1. 'Steynton' crossed through in ms.

169. *St Davids diocese. Answers.*
David Estradu, 'St Kaducus', St Davids diocese: 6s. 8d.

170. *Winchester diocese. Answers.*
William Rode, Shalfleet (Shaldflet): 6s 8d.

171. *Exeter diocese.*
John Cristemasse, Lamorran (Lamorren) in Cornwall.
The prior of Launceston collector answers for this item.

172. *Approval.* Total persons on this roll with whom the aforesaid collector is burdened, beyond other ecclesiastical persons found in the accounts of other collectors, six persons; subsidy £2.

POLL TAX OF 1381 IN THE CITY OF LONDON

173. [E179/42/10a face. Incomplete. Each person is assessed at 3s 4d.]
St Mary Magdalen Milk Street (Melkstrete). Chaplains: John Barbour, William Salman, Andrew, Richard Schalgrave.

174. St Mary Magdalen Old Fish Street. Rector: John Brampton; chaplains: Roger de Holtham, John de Salisbury, Thomas de Henyngham.

175. St Mary Mounthaw. Rector: William Barowe; chaplain: Stephen Walche.

176. St Mary Staining. Rector: John Edward; chaplain: William.

177. St Margaret Fish Street Hill. Rector: Robert; chaplains: John Grantham, Robert Coggeshale, William Horn, John Little.

178. St Margaret Lothbury (Lothebury). Rector: Roger Farndon; chaplains: William Wermyngton, John Borham, Richard Smith, Gilbert Amory.

179. St Margaret Pattens (Patyns). Rector: John.

180. St Margaret Moses Friday Street. Rector: John Fraunceys; chaplains: John Wedon, Nicholas.

181. St Mildred Poultry. Rector: William Pynchebek; chaplains: Robert Sely, Thomas de Muston, John de Broghton.

182. St Mildred Bread Street (Bredstrete). Rector: John Malton; chaplains: John Essex, John Tikhull, John Besewyk, Robert Besewyk, Henry Hothom, John Stormesworthe, John Garforde, William Henry.

183. St Martin Orgar. Rector: William Cestre; chaplains: Richard Mayon, Nicholas Asscheborn.

184. St Martin Ludgate. Rector: John; chaplains: Roger Hake, Robert Clerk, John Mulsham, Laurence Howet, John Rifton (?), Richard Bokbynder.

185. St Martin Vintry. Rector: Roger Lemsterr; chaplains: Thomas Bartlot, Thomas, Walter, John Hoton.

186. St Martin Pomery. Rector: John Redhod; chaplains: Thomas Barowe, John Colyntre, Stephen Benet.

187. St Martin Oteswich. Rector: William; chaplains: Richard, Walter Rous.

188. St Matthew Friday Street. Rector: John Eccleshale; chaplains: William Forneux, John Borgeloun, William Seuster (?), William Meldeborn, Thomas, Richard.

189. St Magnus the Martyr. Rector: Walter; chaplains: Henry, Philip Canoun, Robert Caster (?), John Staunton, Robert Welsokyn, John Lyndiseye, John Cauntirbury, Thomas Howlf.

190. Chapel [of St Thomas the Martyr] on the Bridge. Chaplains: John atte Welle, Walter Coteler, Robert, William.

191. St Nicholas Cole Abbey (Coldabbeye). Rector: John Baude; chaplains: Ralph Donyngton, William Jewel, Robert Pitton, William de Upton, John de Bokyngham, William Algere, John dwelling with the rector.

192. St Nicholas Acon. Rector: William; chaplain: John Haukyn.

193. Total: persons: 93. 92 persons.[1]
      subsidy: £15 10s 0d. £15 10s 0d.[2]
  1. & 2. Total crossed through.

194. [dorse] Hospital (House) of St Thomas Acon. Master: Richard Alred; brothers, domini: Richard Sewell, Laurence Barnet, Nicholas Licchesfeld, Thomas Bakedale, Thomas Wynchecombe, Thomas Ysaak.

195. Abbey of St Mary Graces. Abbot: William de Wardon; monks, brothers: John de Forda, Thomas de Ledis, Richard Passtheneye, Jordan Bikeliswade, Semanius de London, Roger Ykham.

196. Charterhouse. Prior: John; monks, brothers: four called John, two called Robert, Hugh, Richard, Walter, Edmund, Matthew, Peter, Guy; lay brother: Thomas.

197. HOUSE OF THE NUNS OF HALIWELL (Haldwell). Prioress: Anne; nuns, domine: Helen Grosham, Isabel Norton, Joan Hide, Joan Parker, Isabel Causton, Joan Broun, Elizabeth Arundel, Margaret Bernham, Joan Spencer, Joan Pentre, Alice Yonge, Agnes Lymbury.

198. BETHLEHEM HOSPITAL. Master: brother William Tuce.

199. NEW TEMPLE. Master: John Burford.

200. HOUSE OF MINORESSES WITHOUT ALDGATE. Abbess: Eleanor; and twenty-six sisters. Total: £4 10s 0d.
[Damaged] 44(?) persons. £7 6s 8d.

201. Total: persons: 71.
        subsidy: £11 16s 8d.
Approved for allocation at the foot of his account.
The collector asks to be excused from: £4 10s 0d for the said minoress abbess and sisters, under (per) a privy seal writ of 1 March 4 Richard II; [the money due] from Robert Halewey chaplain, under a privy seal writ of 8 March 4 Richard II; [the money due] from Robert Gadham chaplain under a royal writ of 26 February 4 Richard II.

202. Sum total of these two rolls.
Priests, beneficed and unbeneficed, regular and secular: 631.
Subsidy: £211 10s 6d; from each person: 6s 8d.
Whence a surplus (unde de incro'): £1 3s 4d [rectius £1 3s 10d].
Clerks: 34; subsidy: £1 3s 4d, viz. from each person 1s 0d.

POLL TAX OF 1381 IN THE DEANERY OF BOW

203. [E179/42/11 m. 1] London. Particulars of the account of Robert de Bere and Adam Pritewell rectors[1] [of St Michael Paternoster and All Hallows] Lombard Street (Grascherche) London collectors of the subsidy of 6s 8d[2] [. . . from the clergy both beneficed and unbeneficed] regular and secular granted to[3] the king by the clergy in the fourth year [of his reign] in the deanery [of Bow . . .] by the venerable father Simon late archbishop of Canterbury for [. . .]
Rec[eived.]
ST MARY LE BOW (de Arcubus). Rector, John de Tynworth, paying £1 10s; chaplains: Thomas Rouseby, John Peioun; perpetual chaplain: John Sholdham; chaplains: William Lightfoot, John Frend, Robert Baker.

    1. The right hand side of the document is damaged at the top.
    2. '20 groats' in ms. Each chaplain is assessed at 3s 4d, each perpetual chaplain at 6s 8d.
    3. Interlined from here until the next square bracket.

204. [ST MARY] ALDERMARY (Aldermanchirche). Rector, Henry Meddebury, paying £1 10s; perpetual chaplains: Geoffrey de Osmoston, Henry Spencer, John Rache; chaplains: Edmund Walsyngham, Robert de Etton.

27

205. St MICHAEL PATERNOSTER (de Paternosterchirche). Rector, Thomas [sic] de Bere, paying 13s 4d; perpetual chaplains: John Chaumberlayn, Thomas Buk; chaplains: Walter Chircheman, John White.

206. St PANCRAS. Rector, Robert Martyn, paying £1 3s 4d; perpetual chaplains: John Rommeseye, William Sagowe, William Temple; chaplains: John Pleystowe, William Dersyngham; perpetual chaplain: Henry Jolipas.

207. St JOHN THE EVANGELIST. Rector, Edmund Wymundeswold, paying 10s; chaplain: Nicholas de Hanchirche.

208. ALL HALLOWS BREAD STREET. Rector, John Clifton, paying £1 13s 4d; chaplains: William Hoo, Richard Gondeby, Ralph Peykerk, Robert North-borowe, Stephen Kirkstede, Edward Hoper, Thomas Wellendon, John Gueth, William atte Halle.

209. St VEDAST. Rector, John Lynton, paying £1 13s 4d; chaplains: Nicholas Hauley, Hugh Lynton, Thomas de Heghfeld, William Roilund, Thomas Redyng, John Roos, John Clerc.

210. St MARY BOTHAW (Bothehawe). Rector, William Robert, paying £1 3s 4d; chaplains: John Taunton, John Parker, Richard [damaged] rmyn, Robert Barton, John Broke; chaplains of the prior of St Mary Bishopsgate (Bisshopisgate): John, Robert.

211. St LEONARD EASTCHEAP (Estchepe). Rector, Geoffrey de la Launde, paying £1 10s; chaplains: Nicholas Fallardeston, John Weston, John Aston, Richard Baillip, John Levenoth; perpetual chaplain: Elias Archier; chaplain: Thomas Lubry.

212. St MICHAEL CROOKED LANE (Crokedlane). Rector, Roger Peres, paying £1 13s 4d; chaplains: Thomas [damaged] areis, Richard Warmyngton, William Spaldyng, Thomas Sibile, Robert Gloucestre, William Sutton, John Parker, John Taket, John Randolf, Thomas Newton, John Croidon, William Dalyngton, John Kirton.

213. ALL HALLOWS LOMBARD STREET (Graschirche). Rector, Adam de Pritewell, paying 13s 4d; chaplains: Thomas Marchaunt, Roger de Lemie.

214. St DUNSTAN IN THE EAST. [m. 2] Rector, William Islep, paying £2 3s 4d; chaplains: William Melton, Richard Newport, Richard atte Lee, John Baron, Stephen Taunton, Thomas Wodehous, John Fakenham, Robert Donwirth, William Wircestre, Richard Wircestre, John More, John Assh, William Thorn, William Noverton, Thomas Shirbourne, John Dreyton, John Jay, John Mawton.

215. St DIONIS BACKCHURCH. Rector, Henry Robert, paying £1 10s; chaplains: John Preston, William Middleton, Richard Grosby, John Lakynton. Total money as far as here: £34. Approved.

Total persons: 102. Approved.
And so for each person 6s 8d. Approved.

216. Clerks paying 1s each: Thomas Derbi, St Mary Aldermary; William Shirbourne, St Michael Paternoster; Robert Lambard, All Hallows Bread Street; John Pountfree, St Leonard Eastcheap; John Tedeshore [St Michael] Crooked Lane; John Archier, [All Hallows] Lombard Street.
Total money from clerks: 6s. Total persons: 6. This is 1s per clerk. Approved.

POLL TAX OF 1381 IN THE ARCHDEACONRY OF MIDDLESEX

217. [E179/44/347 m. 1] Particulars of the account of the prior of Holy Trinity London collector in the archdeaconry of Middlesex of a subsidy granted by the clergy to the king in the fourth year [of his reign].

[Each person pays 3s 4d unless otherwise stated, except in the case of clerks who invariably pay 1s.]

BRAUGHING DEANERY (Braghwyng).
ROYSTON [PRIORY]. John prior £1 3s 1½d; John (2), Edmund (2), William canons.

218. BARLEY (Berle). John [de Duncryco] rector 11s; William, John celebrants; William clerk.

219. BARKWAY (Berkewey). William [Bunch] vicar 6s 8d; John celebrant; William clerk.

220. REED (Rede). John [Petyt] rector 10s 1½d; John Stacy clerk.

221. BUCKLAND (Bokelond). Richard [Chamberlyn] rector 15s 3½d; William celebrant; Thomas clerk.

222. BIGGIN [HOSPITAL] (Byggyng). William master 16s 4d; William brother.

223. WYDDIAL (Wydiale). James rector 7s 1d.

224. LAYSTON (Leyston). Simon vicar 7s.

225. ALSWICK (Alswyk). Robert celebrant 7s 10d.

226. ANSTEY (Ansty). John rector 8s; William celebrant; William clerk.

227. MEESDON (Mesdon). Richard rector 8s.

228. BRENT PELHAM (Pellam Arsa). Robert vicar 6s 8d.

229. STOCKING PELHAM (Stokpellam). Alexander [Podemey] rector 6s 8d.

230. FURNEUX PELHAM (Pellam Fornwos). John vicar 6s 8d; Robert celebrant; John clerk.

231. ALDBURY (Aldebery). William vicar 7s 9½d; Richard chaplain; John clerk.

232. MUCH HADHAM (Haddam Magna). William rector 16s 10d; John chaplain.

233. LITTLE HADHAM (Haddham Parva). Richard chaplain.

234. BISHOP'S STORTFORD (Storteford). Philip [at Brugg] vicar 6s 8d; Thomas, John celebrants; John clerk.

235. THORLEY (Thorle). John rector 6s 8d; John chaplain.

236. SAWBRIDGEWORTH (Sabriscworth). Thomas[1] vicar 9s; Geoffrey, John celebrants; John, Stephen clerks.
    1. 'John' lightly written above.

237. GILSTON (Gedlaston). Richard [Troubrigge] rector 7s 9d.

238. EASTWICK (Estwyk). John rector 6s 8d.

239. WIDFORD (Wydeford). John [Dykeman] rector 6s 8d.

240. HUNSDON (Honisdone). Thomas rector 7s.

241. STANSTEAD ABBOTS (Stanstede). Henry vicar 8s 2½d.

242. STANSTEAD ST MARGARETS (Thele). Ralph [at Hall] rector 6s 6½d; John[1] celebrant; Thomas clerk.
    1. 'Arnold' written above.

243. BROXBOURNE (Brokesborne). John vicar 6s 5d; Bartholomew celebrant; William clerk.

244. CHESHUNT (Chesthunte). Simon rector 16s 4d; John vicar 6s 8d; Thomas, John celebrants; Thomas clerk.

245. AMWELL. Angerus [Cadeneye] vicar [damaged]; John celebrant.

246. WARE. Philip [Hertford] vicar 7s 6d; John, William, John celebrants; John clerk.

247. THUNDRIDGE (Thundrych). John chaplain.

248. STANDON (Stondon). Thomas vicar 6s 8d; William, John chaplains; Thomas clerk.

249. BRAUGHING. Robert vicar 7s 9d; Adam celebrant; Geoffrey clerk.

250. LITTLE HORMEAD (Hormed Parva). John[1] rector 6s 5d.
  1. 'William' written above [perhaps William Hornby].

251. GREAT HORMEAD (Hormed Magna). Nicholas [at Lane] vicar 6s 8d.

252. [m. 2] Approved. Total chaplains: 66.
  subsidy: £20 6s 11½d.
  clerks: 16.
  subsidy: 16s.

253. HEDINGHAM DEANERY (Hityngham).
[Unheaded]: John celebrant; Richard parochial chaplain.

254. CASTLE HEDINGHAM (Hengham Castre). John, William celebrants; Agnes prioress; Katherine subprioress; Margaret, Margery, Alice sisters.

255. HALSTEAD (Halstede). Robert vicar 6s 4d; Robert, Richard celebrants; Richard clerk.

256. GESTINGTHORPE (Gestyngthorp). William rector 6s 4d; Richard vicar 7s; John clerk.

257. BELCHAMP WALTER (Bewchamp Simonis). Richard vicar 7s 9½d; Robert clerk.

258. BELCHAMP OTTON (Belchampot'). John rector 7s; John celebrant; John clerk.

259. OVINGTON (Ovintone). Robert rector 6s 9½d.

260. PENTLOW (Pentelowe). Roger rector 8s ½d; Peter celebrant.

261. FOXEARTH (Foxherde). John rector 5s 6½d.

262. LISTON (Lyston). Walter rector 6s 2½d.

263. BORLEY (Borle). William rector 7s; Richard celebrant.

264. BALLINGDON CUM BRUNDON[1] (Brondone). James [Thyrlowe] rector 7s 5d.
  1. Now in Suffolk.

265. BULMER (Bulmere). Nicholas [de Fladbury] rector 15s 8d; John celebrant.

266. MIDDLETON (Middilton). John rector 7s 3d.

267. LITTLE HENNY (Heney Parva). Hugh rector 7s 5d.

268. GREAT HENNY (Heney Magna). Andrew [Gerard] rector 5s 5d; William celebrant.

269. LAMARSH (Lamersch). John [Litele] rector 6s 8d.

270. ALPHAMSTONE (Alfhampston). Alan rector 6s 5d.

271. PEBMARSH (Pebemerch). John [Wayte] rector 6s 11d. Henry celebrant; Roger clerk.

272. LITTLE MAPLESTEAD (Mapelstede Parva). Richard parochial chaplain.

273. GREAT MAPLESTEAD (Mapilstede Magna). John vicar 6s 1d.

274. SIBLE HEDINGHAM (Hengham Sibil). John [Stanfeld] rector 6s 5½d; John celebrant; Thomas clerk.

275. GOSFIELD (Goffeld). Adam vicar 8s 6¼d; Richard celebrant; William clerk.

276. SHALFORD (Schaldeford). William vicar 7s 5d; Robert celebrant; William clerk.

277. GREAT SALING (Salyng). John vicar 6s 7d.

278. STEBBING (Stebbyng). John vicar 6s 3½d; William celebrant; Robert clerk.

279. FINCHINGFIELD (Fynchingfeld). John vicar 11s 2d; Robert, John celebrants; Alexander clerk.

280. STEEPLE BUMPSTEAD (Bumstede). John [Miskham] vicar 5s 9d; Geoffrey clerk.

281. STURMER (Starmere). John rector 6s.

282. BIRDBROOK (Brydbroke). John rector 8s 4d; John celebrant.

283. STAMBOURNE (Stanborne). Richard [Goderam] rector 6s 2d; John celebrant.

284. RIDGEWELL (Radiswelle). John vicar 7s 5d.

285. TOPPESFIELD (Topisfeld). John rector 7s 6d; Stephen vicar 5s 4d; John celebrant.

32

286. GREAT YELDHAM (Gelham Magna). Richard rector 9s 8d.

287. LITTLE YELDHAM (Gelham Parva). John [Hervy] rector 6s 4d; John celebrant.

288. WICKHAM ST PAUL'S (Wyham Paul). Thomas rector 5s 5½d; Roger clerk.

289. PANFIELD (Pandefeld). Robert rector 7s 10d.

290. RAYNE (Reynes Parva). Richard [de Orcheston] rector 9s 2d; John celebrant.

291. BRAINTREE (Reynes Magna). John [Champayne] rector 11s 8d; Thomas vicar 7s 5d; Gervaise celebrant.

292. WETHERSFIELD (Werisfeld). Thomas rector 6s 5½d; Thomas, Richard celebrants; William[1] clerk.
    1. 'Thomas' interlined.

293. TILBURY-JUXTA-CLARE (Tilbery). Robert [Lyrycocke] rector 6s 3½d; Edmund celebrant.

294. TWINSTEAD (Twynstede). N [sic] rector 8s 8d.

295. Approved. Total chaplains: 75.
                subsidy: £20 19s 2½d.
                [m. 3] clerks: 13.
                subsidy: 13s.

296. DUNMOW DEANERY (Donmowe).
TILTY [ABBEY] (Tyltey). William abbot 14s 4½d; Clement, John, Thomas, John (2), William monks.

297. DUNMOW [PRIORY]. John [de Swafham] prior 16s 4d; John, Stephen, Henry, Edmund, Thomas, John (2), Thomas, Henry canons.

298. GOOD EASTER (Godestre). John vicar 6s 9d.

299. THAXTED (Thaxstede). Thomas celebrant [sic] 9s 8d; Robert (2), William celebrants; Robert, John clerks.

300. GREAT DUNMOW (Donmowe Magna). John [de Capell] rector 11s 2d; William celebrant; John [Spicer] vicar 8s 10d; William Bette celebrant; John Herry, John Brydd clerks.

301. FELSTEAD (Felstede). John vicar 8s; Robert celebrant; John clerk.

302. BARNSTON (Bermston). William rector 4s 8d.

303. PLESHEY (Plesch'). John vicar 7s 4d; Robert celebrant; John clerk.

304. HIGH EASTER (Alta Estre). John vicar 8s.

305. MASHBURY (Maschbery). Richard rector 9s.

306. SHELLOW BOWELLS (Schelwe). Richard rector 6s 8d.

307. WILLINGALE DOE (Wylinghale Do). John rector 7s.

308. WILLINGALE SPAIN (Wilinghaleand'). William [Beverage] rector 7s.

309. BERNERS RODING (Rothingberners). Roger chaplain 5s.

310. MARGARET RODING (Rothingmerger'). William [Stacy] rector 7s 8d.

311. LEADEN RODING (Rothingplumbea). Richard rector 5s 5½d; John chaplain.

312. WHITE RODING (Rothing Alba). Richard rector 15s.

313. AYTHORPE RODING (Rothingaytorpe). John rector 4s 8d; Richard Coventre.

314. HIGH RODING (Rothing Alta). Richard rector 13s 1d; John Crespyn celebrant.

315. GREAT CANFIELD (Canfeld Magna). Thomas vicar 7s 9½d; John clerk.

316. LITTLE CANFIELD (Canfeld Parva). John Ansty rector 5s 5d; John clerk.

317. LITTLE EASTON (Eston Parva). John [Brunne] rector 5s 5d.

318. LINDSELL (Lyndesele). John vicar 6s.

319. WIMBISH (Wymbich). John celebrant.

320. CHICKNEY (Chakeneye). John rector 7s 9½d; Robert celebrant.

321. BROXTED [CHAURETH] (Chaurer). William vicar 7s 5d; William clerk.

322. Approved. Total chaplains: 53.
                 subsidy: £15 5s 6d.
                 clerks: 9.
                 subsidy: 9s.

323. HARLOW DEANERY (Herlawe).
HATFIELD [PRIORY] (Hatfeld). John prior 13s 5d; John subprior; Roger, Nicholas, Bartholomew, John, William canons.

324. HATFIELD BROAD OAK (Hatfeld Regis). John vicar 8s; Thomas, John (2) celebrants; Richard, William clerks.

325. [m. 4] HARLOW (Herlowe). William [de Humberston] rector 13s 4d; John chaplain; William celebrant.

326. SHEERING (Scheryng). Ralph [Harpele] rector 9s 8d; John celebrant.

327. MATCHING (Machyng). John Northyn vicar 5s 3½d; William celebrant.

328. LATTON [PRIORY] (Lattone). Peter prior 6s 8d; William vicar.

329. NETTESWELL (Nettliswell). Ralph rector 7s 9½d.

330. GREAT PARNDON (Pendon Magna). Thomas rector 5s.

331. LITTLE PARNDON (Pendon Parva). For which John Northyn [pays] 6s.

332. ROYDON (Reydon). Richard [Wokking] vicar 7s; William with lady Tiptot.

333. GREAT HALLINGBURY (Halingbury Magna). Robert rector 6s 6d; John celebrant.

334. LITTLE HALLINGBURY (Halingbury Parva). William rector 5s 11½d.

335. Approved. Total chaplains: 28.
          subsidy: £7 7s 11½d.
          clerks: 2.
          subsidy: 2s.

336. MIDDLESEX DEANERY (Middilsex).
OGBOURNE [PRIORY][1] (Okeborne). Prior £1 18s 10d; Philip vicar 9s 6d.
   1. Not conventual.

337. HARMONDSWORTH [PRIORY] (Hermedesworth). Richard prior £1 18s 3d; John vicar; John brother.

338. STANWELL. Richard [de Thorp] rector 19s 2d; Richard vicar 5s 8d; Robert clerk.

339. SHEPPERTON (Scheperton). Thomas rector 7s; Peter celebrant.

340. LITTLETON? (Litchyngton). Peter rector 11s 5d; William celebrant.

341. HARLINGTON (Herdyngton). John rector 6s.

342. HILLINGDON (Hylingdon). William vicar 6s 8d; William celebrant; Thomas clerk.

343. COWLEY (Couele). John rector 6s.

344. ICKENHAM (Ikynham). John [de Brokhampton] rector 8s.

345. NORTHOLT (Northalle). Thomas vicar 7s.

346. GREENFORD (Grenford Magna). John rector 5s ½d.

347. PERIVALE (Grenford Parva). Edmund [Letys] rector 7s 5d.

348. STANMORE (Stanmere). Thomas [Strete] rector 7s 6½d.

349. HENDON. Thomas [de Evere or Eure] rector 17s 10d; Thomas vicar 9s; John celebrant.

350. ST CLEMENT DANES (Clement London). William rector 7s 8d.

351. STRAND (Stronde). John rector 18s 1d; Richard celebrant.

352. ST MARTIN IN THE FIELDS (Martin in Campo). John vicar 3s 4d.

353. CHELSEA (Chelcheth). Richard rector 11s 6½d; John clerk.

354. ACTON. Richard [de Pertenhale] rector 7s; William celebrant; John clerk.

355. STEPNEY (Stebenheth). Robert [Crull] rector £1 6s 2d; Nicholas [Dene] vicar 11s 2d; John celebrant; John clerk.

356. FULHAM. William [de Shirbourne or Ilberd] rector £1 7s 11½d; John vicar 6s 3½d; Nicholas celebrant.

357. HACKNEY (Hakyneye). Thomas [de Myddleton] rector £1 6s 4d; Roger [Slatburn] vicar; John clerk.

358. HANWORTH. John [Bakere] rector 5s 8d.

359. BEDFONT (Bedefont). Alan [Shodington] vicar 6s.

360. FELTHAM. John vicar 7s. 4d.

361. STAINES (Stanis). Thomas [Gilmyn] vicar 6s 2d; William clerk.

362. KENSINGTON. William vicar 15s 7d.

363. ISLEWORTH? (Killworth). Laurence vicar 7s 9d.

364. TWICKENHAM (Twykinham). Michael [de Shires] vicar 6s 10d.

365. CRANFORD. Henry [Casse] rector 7s 10d.

366. STRATFORD-AT-BOW [PRIORY] (Strattford). Mary [Suharde] prioress; Felicity subprioress; Julia, Joan, Argentina, Joan, Isabel, Joan, Alice, Letitia, Alice, Margaret, Katherine, Margaret nuns.

367. [m. 5] BRENTFORD (Braynford). John rector 17s 3d.

368. HARRINGAY (Haringeye). Ralph rector 7s 9d.

369. FINCHLEY (Fynchisley). John rector 7s 9d.

370. TYBURN (Tyborne). William chaplain.

371. ENFIELD (Enefeld). John [de Ekyndon] vicar 8s 10d; John, William celebrants.

372. TOTTENHAM (Totenham). John vicar 6s; William clerk.

373. EALING (Jellyng). Richard vicar 7s.

374. CHISWICK. John vicar 8s 4d.

375. HOUNSLOW (Houndeslowe). Brother William minister; Simon, Geoffrey, Robert brothers.

376. HAREFIELD (Herefeld). Philip chaplain.

377. MONKEN HADLEY[1] (Manncherche). John chaplain.
  1. Now in Hertfordshire.

378. HESTON (Eston). John vicar 6s 5d.

379. HAMPTON (Hamptone). Richard [Mansell] vicar 6s 2d.

380. SUNBURY (Sunnebery). Richard vicar 7s 4d; Thomas celebrant.

381. LALEHAM. William vicar 5s 2d.

382. SOUTH MIMMS (Southmimys). Richard vicar 6s 2d.

383. WILLESDEN (Wilisden). Thomas vicar 8s 2d.

384. EDGWARE (Egiswere). Walter celebrant.

385. WHITCHURCH (Stanmere Parva). William celebrant 6s 8d.

386. KINGSBURY (Kyngisbery). Richard celebrant 5s 8d.

387. St Giles Hospital [Holborn]. Brother William [Croxton] master 6s 8d; Nicholas brother; William, Henry celebrants.

388. Kilburn [Priory] (Kylborn). Alice prioress; Katherine, Maud, Margery, Emma, Margaret nuns.

389. St John Hospital. Brother John; Roger, Adam, William.

390. Westminster [Abbey]. Nicholas [Litlington] abbot £14 13s 4d; John Exeter, John Mirymuth, Walter Warefeld, William Mordon, John Wrattyng, Richard Chichestre, Robert Hereford, John Stowe, William Colchestre, John Lagyngheth, John Ovyngton, John Catisbery, John Faringho, William Lythington, Peter Cowmbe, John Gyffard, William Wittlisford, Roger Denham, Thomas Warwyk, Richard Merlawe, Robert Athelard, Bartholomew London, Nicholas Cherynton, Thomas Pomfreyt, John London, John Sutton, Richard Palgrave, John Sandon.

391. St Margaret Westminster. William parochial chaplain; Simon, William, Nicholas, John celebrants; Thomas clerk.

392. St James Hospital. Thomas Orgrave master [damaged]; Nicholas Weston, Roger, Nicholas, Thomas celebrants.

393. The King's Chapel at Westminster. William Sleford dean £1 1s; John Corby, Thomas Orgrave, Nicholas Salesbery, Ralph Kesteyn, Thomas Midilton, John Henle, Robert Derby, William Wenlok, William Beverle, Richard Clifford, John Welyngboruth canons paying 9s each; William Dedynton, William Mayn, Henry Wynchestre, [m. 6] John Warwyk, Thomas Grantham, John Hespley, John Cassell, William Holstret, John Mauntoft, Thomas Exstede, Thomas Oefford vicars.

394. Approved. Total persons regular and secular: 162.
> subsidy: £64 4s ½d.[1]
> clerks: 9s.
> subsidy: 9s.

1. '½d' crossed out.

395. Approved. Sum total persons secular and regular: 384.
> subsidy: £128[1] viz. from each person 6s 8d.
> clerks: 49.
> subsidy: £2 9s viz. from each person 1s.

Approved. Sum total received £130 9s.[2]

1. '17s 5d' and '14s 4d' crossed out.
2. 'Sum total received £127 13s 4d' crossed out.

ECCLESIASTICAL PROPERTY IN THE CITY OF LONDON, 1392

(Corporation of London Records Office, 239A)

[An assessment of rents and a calculation thereon of 40d in the pound are given but the latter is here omitted.]

396. [m. 1] BROAD STREET WARD.
PARISH OF ST BARTHOLOMEW [BY THE EXCHANGE].
Rents of the abbot of St Mary Graces (Tourhill) £11 14s 4d.
Quit rents from the tenements of: Walter Newynton to the nuns of St Helen £7 0s 0d; Richard Sturry kt to the church of St Bartholomew 10s 0d.
Rents of the prior of Canterbury £11 16s 8d.
Quit rents from the tenements of: John Humbre to the abbot of Westminster 3s 0d; Margaret Wallworth to the abbot of St Mary Graces £1 5s 0d; John Pyel to the abbot of St Albans 8s 0d; the said John to the prior of Merton 4s 0d; Margaret Cok to the church of St Paul 2s 0d; Bartholomew Bosham to the prioress of St Helen £2 5s 0d; Alice Lyndewyk to the hospital of St James 2s 1d.

397. PARISH OF ST BENET FINK.
Rents of the archdeacon of Colchester £14 0s 0d; his tenement which John Clee holds £2 0s 0d.
Rents of: the abbot of St Mary Graces £7 17s 4d; the abbot of St Albans £15 13s 4d; the fraternity of St John £5 8s 0d.
Quit rent from the tenement which Helen Kilpyn holds of the Austin friars of London £11 0s 0d.
Rents of the archdeacon of Colchester £4 0s 0d; from his tenement to the church of St Paul 13s 4d.

398. PARISH OF ST MARGARET [LOTHBURY].
Rents of: the church of St Dionis £3 10s 0d; the abbot of St Mary Graces £6 0s 8d.
From the tenement which Ed[mund] Hoddesdon holds to a chantry in St Margaret Lothbury church £6 0s 0d.
Quit rent from the tenement of Joan Thirlowe to the house of St Bartholomew 6s 0d.

399. PARISH OF ST CHRISTOPHER.
Quit rent from the tenements of: Margaret Wallworth to [blank] Hardyngham friar preacher £1 0s 0d; lady de Nevyle to the church of St Christopher 15s 11d.

Rents of: the prior of Charterhouse £13 6s 8d; the rector of the church of St Christopher £2 0s 0d.

Quit rents from the tenements of: Thomas Wodehouse to the church of St Antonin 15s 0d; Adam Carlehill to the church of St Christopher 9s 3d.

Rents of: the church of St Lawrence Pountney (Pulteneye) £1 0s 0d; the rector of the church of St Christopher £2 0s 0d.

Quit rents from the tenement of Thomas Hauton to the prioress of Haliwell 8s 0d.

400. Parish of St Mary Woolchurch (Wolchirchehawe).

Quit rents from the tenement of Thomas Hore to the said church of St Mary £4 0s 0d.

Tenement of the rector of St Mary Woolchurch. *Chantry* £6 0s 0d.

Quit rent from the tenement of Benedict Cornwaille to the abbot of Reading (Redyng) 13s 0d.

401. Parish of St Peter le Poor.

Quit rent from the tenement of Maud Holbeche to the nuns of St Helen 15s 0d; from her tenement to the rector All Hallows London Wall 1s 0d.

Rents of: the nuns of St Helen £10 0s 0d; the church of St Botolph Billingsgate (Billingesgate) £3 6s 8d; the abbot of St Albans £8 18s 0d; the rector of the church of St Peter £1 6s 6d; the Austin friars London £22 0s. 0d.

Quit rents from the tenement of Maud Holbeche to the nuns of St Helen £1 18s 4d.

402. Parish of St Martin Oteswich (Oteswyche).

Quit rent from the tenement of John Wakeley to the prior of Holy Trinity Aldgate (Chrichirche) 15s 0d; from the tenement of the same John to the nuns of St Helen 9s 8d.

Quit rents from the tenements of: Henry Yeveley to the nuns of Stratford-at-Bow 18s 8d; Richard Hervy to the prior of Holy Trinity 4s 0d; John Chircheman to the prior of the Charterhouse £2 0s 0d.

Rents of the prioress of Cheshunt £1 13s 0d.

403. Parish of All Hallows London Wall.

Quit rent from the tenement of sir Robert Bardolf [blank] of St Bartholomew 3s 0d; from his tenement to the prior of Holy Trinity 1s 7d; from the said tenement to the church of St Katherine 10s 0d.

Quit rent from the tenement of Richard Cok to the hospital of St Mary without Bishopsgate 13s 4d.

Rents of the prior of the hospital of St Mary without Bishopsgate £1 13s 4d.

Quit rents from the tenements of: Nicholas Cok to the hospital of St James 16s 6d; Stephen Baron to the nuns of St Helen 5s 0d; from the same tenement to the rector [sic] of St Mary aforesaid 3s 0d.

Quit rent from the tenement of William Derby to the hospital of St Mary without Bishopsgate 10s 0d; from the same tenement [blank] of St Bartholomew 2s 0d.

Quit rents from the tenements of: the wife of Henry Treynell to the nuns of Haliwell 15s 0d; William Belham to the nuns of Haliwell 2s 0d.

404. PARISH OF ST MILDRED POULTRY.
Quit rent from the tenement of Adam Bamme to the church of St Mildred 10s 0d.

405. [m. 1d] CANDLEWICK STREET WARD (Candelwykstret).
[The entries for this ward are duplicated, with a few additions, on m. 8d; see **501**].

PARISH OF ST MARY ABCHURCH (Abbechirche).
From the tenement of John Basse to St Mary Abchurch £1 6s 8d.
Rents of: the prior of Newark (Newerk) £3 6s 8d; the prior of Hitchin (Huchene) which John Basse holds p.a. £8 0s 0d.
Three shops of the minoresses next the Tower of London worth p.a. £4 0s 0d.
Tenement of the prioress of Clerkenwell worth p.a. £2 0s 0d.
From the tenements: which John Abel holds to the prioress of Cheshunt 2s 6d; of John Walcote formerly of Adam Crafte to the prioress of Haliwell 12s 0d; of Richard Bedewynd to the prior of Bermondsey (Bermondeseye) 8s 0d; of the prior of Elsing Spital which John Gyle holds £6 10s 0d; which Bartholomew Neve and Reginald atte Pole hold to the prior of Holy Trinity £2 13s 4d; which John Campion, William Halton, Richard Spencer and William Horwode hold to the prior of Holy Trinity £3 0s 0d; from the same tenement to the prior of Merton 5s 0d; which Robert Brisele holds to the prior of Elsing Spital £3 13s 4d; which William Norton holds to the prior of Southwark (St Mary Overy) 6s 8d.

406. PARISH OF ST CLEMENT [EASTCHEAP].
Quit rents of the tenements: of Andrew Pybaker to the abbot of Westminster 2s 0d; which John Pope holds to the prior of Elsing Spital 9s 0d; the same tenement to a chantry in the church of St Paul 13s 4d; of John Parker to the prior of Elsing Spital 10s 0d; from the same tenements to the prior of Southwark 6s 0d; of Avice (?) Tonge which Henry Edward, Elias Broun, William Barker hold to the rector of St Margaret Fish Street Hill (bridge) £3 0s 0d.
Memorandum. Rents of the prior of Elsing Spital £6 0s 0d.

407. PARISH OF ST LEONARD EASTCHEAP.
From the tenement of the church of St Mary at Hill (Hulle) which William Barker holds £2 0s 0d.
Quit rent from the tenement which Richard Michewyk and Richard Cheseman hold to the church of St Leonard £3 0s 0d.
Rents of the prior of Elsing Spital which Thomas Sampson holds £2 0s 0d.
Quit rent from the tenements of John Doget to the church of St Matthew Friday Street (Fridaystrete) £2 0s 0d.
Rent of the prior of St Mary without Bishopsgate which Thomas atte Hole holds £1 6s 8d.

41

Quit rents from the tenements of: Robert Lyndewyk to the prior of Newark 10s 0d; John Edward to the prioress of Kilburn (Kylbourne) 11s 0d.

408. PARISH OF ST MICHAEL CROOKED LANE.
Four shops which the butchers hold in Eastcheap to the college of St Michael Crooked Lane £10 0s 0d; for an inn and two shops at the Fleurdelys (le Flourdelys) to the same £6 13s 4d; divers shops in Crooked Lane belonging to the same £4 0s 0d.
Rents of sir Richard Kyngeston clerk £4 13s 4d.
Quit rents: from the tenements which sir Brouderere holds p.a. to the same college £12 0s 0d; of Hugh Martyn to the same £2 0s 0d.
Rents: of the same college[1] £5 0s 0d; of the same college in St Michael's Lane[2] £1 0s 0d.
Quit rents from the tenements: of Alice Tonge to the prioress of Haliwell 15s 0d; which John Jurdein holds to the prior of the hospital of St Mary without Bishopsgate £1 0s 0d; of Roger atte Sterre £1 0s 0d; aforesaid to the prior of Christ Church Canterbury (Caunterbury) 4s 0d.

1. The entry on m. 8d adds, 'where the chaplains of the college live'.
2. The entry on m. 8d adds, 'which a chaplain holds'.

409. PARISH OF ST MARTIN ORGAR.
Rents of: the prioress of Stratford-at-Bow to a chantry in the church of St Martin Orgar £4 0s 0d; the chapel of Colney worth p.a. 14s 0d; St James Garlickhithe (Garlekhith) church which John Lumbard holds £2 13s 4d; the church of St Martin Orgar £1 0s 0d.
Quit rents from the tenements of: the prioress of Stratford-at-Bow to the prior of Holy Trinity 6s 8d; Thomas Bolfe and Thomas Buk to the prior of Merton £2 3s 4d. From the same tenement to: the prior of Holy Trinity 7s 0d; the prior of the hospital of St Mary without Bishopsgate 3s 4d; to the prior of Bermondsey 2s 2d.
Rents of the prior of Elsing Spital which William Goryng holds £4 13s 4d.
Quit rent from the tenement of Elias Bokkyng to the prioress of Ankerwyke £2 0s 0d; from the same to the prioress of Clerkenwell £1 6s 8d.
Quit rents from: a tenement of William Oxenford to the prior of Southwark £1 6s 8d; a tenement in the care (spectant') of the church of St Martin Orgar to the prioress of Clerkenwell 12s 0d; a tenement of Hugh Trot to the church of St Martin le Grand 6s 8d; a tenement of John Shordiche to the prioress of Markyate £1 0s 0d; from his tenement to the church of St Martin Orgar 15s 0d; the same to the prior of Southwark 6s 8d.
Quit rent from the tenement of Richard Radwell to the prior of Holy Trinity 14s 0d; from the same to the prior of Bermondsey 10s 0d.

410. PARISH OF ST LAWRENCE POUNTNEY.
Rents of: the church of St Swithin £5 6s 8d; the college of St Lawrence Pountney which Bartholomew Neve holds £2 13s 4d; the same which Robert Fulmere holds £2 13s 4d.

411. FARRINGDON WARD WITHOUT (Farndon).
The church of St Paul: tenements of the dean and chapter which Richard

Haydok and others hold £13 6s 8d; tenement of the same which Roger Rabas and others hold £8 0s 0d; the dove-cote without the bar (le Culu'hous extra barram) belongs to the church £1 0s 0d; rents of William Dyer to the church £2 0s 0d; tenement of the dean £2 0s 0d; the tenement of William Colyn to the church £10 0s 0d.

From the tenements of: the prior of Rochester (Rouchestre) £9 10s 6d; the abbot of Winchcomb (Wynchecombe) £5 6s 8d; the prior of Rochester £4 3s 4d; the dean and chapter of the king's chapel Westminster £1 16s 0d; the same £6 13s 4d.

Rents of the prior of Westminster £1 0s 0d.

412. Shops of the bishop of St Davids (Seint David) £1 16s 0d.

Tenements of: the abbot of Faversham (Feversham) £3 6s 8d; mr Henry Bowet £16 6s 8d; the prioress of Godstow (Godstowe) £2 0s 0d.

Shops of the bishop of Salisbury (Salesbury) £9 13s 4d.

Tenements of: the abbot of St Mary Graces £2 13s 4d; the same £8 0s 0d; the abbot of Peterborough (Petirburgh) £7 3s 4d; the abbot of Warden (Wardon) £2 13s 4d; the prioress of Ankerwyke £10 0s 0d; the abbot of Rewley (Riall') £10 16s 0d; the abbot of Cirencester (Circestre) £6 13s 4d; sir William Ermyn chaplain £20 0s 0d.

413. Tenements of: Thomas atte Wode to the prior of Holy Trinity 6s 0d; the same to the hospital of St James 8s 0d.

Shops of the master of the hospital of St James £1 0s 0d.

From the tenements of: Roger Payn to Elsing Spital £1 6s 8d; the prior and convent of Elsing Spital 13s 4d; John Canon to the house of sisters of Dartford, Kent £3 6s 8d; the prior of Elsing Spital £1 0s 0d; John Fairhode to the priory of Merton 4s 0d; the abbot of Malmesbury £6 0s 0d; the abbot of Burnham £1 0s 0d; *Elye* the bishop of Ely £12 0s 0d; the same £17 6s 8d.

414. Rents of: the prior of Southwark £2 0s 0d; the same £6 13s 4d.

From tenements of: the bishop of Lincoln (Lyncoll') £1 0s 0d; the master of St Giles £1 0s 0d; the same £1 0s 0d.

From shops of the prioress of Clerkenwell £1 8s 0d.

From tenements of: the prior of Sempringham (Symprinham) £14 6s 8d; the abbot of Leicester (Leycestre) £3 0s 0d; the prior of Burton upon Trent £3 6s 8d; the abbot of Thame £4 0s 0d; the dean of Chichester £1 0s 0d; the bishop of Chichester £2 0s 0d; the abbot of Osney £5 6s 8d; the abbot of Leicester £12 0s 0d; sir John Segevawse £6 0s 0d.

415. FROM RENTS TO THE MASTER OF THE HOSPITAL OF ST BARTHOLOMEW SMITHFIELD (Westsmythfeld).

Note. From a tenement £1 0s 0d; from another £1 6s 8d; from another £4 6s 8d.

From: five shops £1 15s 0d; four shops £2 0s 0d.

From a tenement £20 0s 0d; from another £1 6s 8d.

From shops £1 13s 4d.

From a tenement £2 0s 0d; from another with two shops £5 6s 8d; from a house 6s 8d.

From four shops £2 13s 4d.

From a tenement £3 0s 0d; from another £5 0s 0d; from another with five shops £10 10s 0d; from three shops with a house £1 2s 0d.

From rents £3 0s 0d.

416. FROM RENTS, TENEMENTS AND SHOPS OF THE PRIOR OF ST BARTHOLOMEW SMITHFIELD.

From a tenement of the priory £4 0s 0d; from another 18s 0d; from another £2 13s 4d.

From: two shops of the prior £1 0s 0d; three shops £1 6s 8d; a tenement £2 13s 4d; another £1 0s 0d; another £4 0s 0d; four shops £2 0s 0d; twenty shops £9 0s 0d; a tenement £2 0s 0d; another £1 6s 8d; an inn £4 13s 4d; a tenement with ten shops £6 0s 0d; a tenement with six shops £5 0s 0d; two shops 16s 0d.

417. From the tenement of the prior of Royston (Roiston) £6 13s 4d.

Rents of: the Carmelite friars £20 0s 0d; the master of the [New] Temple £40 0s 0d;[1] the prior of St John in the parish of St Sepulchre £12 0s 0d; the abbot of Quenington (Quenyndon) £3 6s 8d; the master of Bridgewater (Briggewater) £2 0s 0d; the church of St Dunstan in the West [blank].

£453 15s 6d.

1. The taxation column has 6s 8d.

418. BILLINGSGATE WARD.

From the tenements of: Henry Boseworth to the prior of Tortington 4s 6d; Gilbert Maghfield to the prior of Holy Trinity £1 2s 0d; *without* John Sybyle to the abbot of Waltham £1 6s 8d; John Wroth to the prior of Bermondsey (Bermundeseye) £2 0s 0d; John Pountfreit to the prior of Southwark 5s 0d; William Reynwell to the abbot of Waltham £1 0s 0d; the same William to the church of St Paul £1 0s 0d; the Charterhouse £5 0s 0d; John Wynter to the prior of Southwark 9s 0d; Wallworth therefrom [blank]; William Burton [blank]; mr Adam Holm £5 0s 0d.

419. From the tenements of: the church of St Botolph £8 0s 0d; John Chambre to the church of St Botolph £4 0s 0d; from the same tenements to the prior of Southwark 13s 4d; Henry Boseworth to the prioress of Cheshunt £2 0s 0d; from the same tenements to the church of St Botolph 3s 4d; Geoffrey Maghfeld to the prior of Holy Trinity 13s 4d; the prioress of St Helen £10 13s 4d; William Bys to the abbot of Waltham £1 5s 8d; Robert Langedon to the same £1 2s 0d; Hugh Schort to the same £1 18s 0d; from the same tenements to the church of St Paul £2 6s 8d; Margaret Walworth to the abbot of Waltham £2 0s 0d; from the same tenements to the prior of Bermondsey 3s 4d.

420. From the tenements of: John Wade to the church of St Mary at Hill

£5 8s 8d; Hugh Schort to the abbey of Waltham £1 6s 8d; from the same tenements to the church of St George £4 6s 8d; William Eynesham to the abbot of Waltham £1 6s 8d; Margaret Walworth to the church of St Mary at Hill 3s 4d; Rose Bysouthe to the abbot of Waltham 13s 4d; John Wade to the church of St Mary at Hill £1 0s 0d; Gilbert Maghfeld to the abbot of Waltham 13s 4d; the prior of Holy Trinity £4 13s 4d; *memorandum* lady de Criell £5 13s 4d; Hugh de Middelton to the abbot of Waltham 13s 4d.

421. From the tenements of: *memorandum* Robert Knolles [blank]; John Wade to Elsing Spital 6s 0d; the abbot of St Mary Graces £2 0s 0d; Richard Maykyn to the church of St Katherine 13s 4d; John Horn to the abbot of Westminster £1 0s 0d; Alice Doget to a chapel in the church of St Leonard Eastcheap £3 6s 8d; from the rector of the same church 8s 0d; the same church for a chantry £3 6s 8d; the church of St Bartholomew £7 10s 0d; the church of St Paul £10 10s 4d; Simon Lemman to the church of St Andrew Hubbard 2s 4d; from the same tenements to the prior of Elsing Spital 5s 0d.

422. From the tenements of: Richard Odyham for a *chantry* £4 16s 8d; Adam Bamme to the church of St Lawrence Pountney £1 0s 0d; Richard Odyham to the prior of Holy Trinity 1s 6d; from the same tenements to the prioress of St Helen 17s 4d; from the same to the church of St Martin Orgar 5s 0d; from the same to the abbot of St Mary Graces £8 1s 0d; the rector of the church of St Christopher £8 0s 2d; Nicholas Dapriscourt to the church of St Katherine 17s 0d; John Picard to the abbot of Waltham 8s 8d; William Barnaby to the prior of Holy Trinity 1s 0d; Richard Tangeley to the said hospital 1s 0d; Andrew Vyne to the hospital of St Mary without Bishopsgate 5s 0d; the church of St Lawrence Pountney £4 13s 4d.

423. From the tenements of: Thomas Mokkyng to the church of St Margaret Fish Street Hill 6s 8d; Geoffrey Maghfeld to the same church 1 lb. of incense; the same Gilbert to the same church 6s 8d; Hugh Schort to the hospital of St Bartholomew 16s 8d; Letitia Fulham to the church of St Margaret 18s 0d; the church of St Paul £1 4s 0d; *without*, the hospital of St Mary without Bishopsgate £8 0s 0d; the church of St Paul £2 0s 0d; the church of St George £4 0s 0d; the church of St Paul £4 0s 0d; the Charterhouse £2 13s 4d.

£152 10s 2d.

424. [m. 3]¹ BRIDGE WARD.
From the tenements of: John Clonnyll of Essex formerly of Richard Blomvill [blank] Clerkenwell 10s 0d; the master of St Lawrence Pountney £1 16s 0d, of which 9s 0d is paid to Clerkenwell.
From [blank] Clerkenwell for two tenements of John Brokhalle chandler which Henry Taillour and Thomas Taillour hold 8s 4d.
From two cottages of Richard Radwell 5s 0d.

From a tenement of: William atte Lee [blank] Clerkenwell 10s 0d; Richard Grace to the nuns of Dartford £1 0s 0d; Richard Radwelle[2] to the church of St Martin Orgar 8s 0d; Richard Radwelle[3] to the hospital of St Giles 8s 0d; John Walworth vintner which Richard Abel holds to the church of St Michael Crooked Lane 6s 8d; the church of St Michael Crooked Lane which John Sewale holds £8 0s 0d, of which 5s 0d p.a. is paid to Bermondsey; the master of the college of St Lawrence Pountney which Laurence Lubenham holds £20 0s 0d, of which £1 0s 0d is paid to Southwark priory, and £14 0s 0d is paid to three chaplains in St Pauls.

1. This membrane is extensively corrected in another hand.
2. The name of the church is crossed through.
3. The name of the hospital is crossed through.

425. PARISH OF ST MICHAEL CROOKED LANE.

From a tenement of: the church of St Michael Crooked Lane which William atte Lee holds £6 13s 4d, of which 14s 0d p.a. is paid to the prior of Southwark, and 10s 0d is paid to the prioress of Clerkenwell; Richard Radwelle to the church of St Michael Crooked Lane two torches.

From the tenements of Margaret Walworth to the same church £4 0s 0d.

From a tenement of: Richard Bedewynde to the prior of Holy Trinity 2s 10d; Thomas Wyght to the church of St Michael Crooked Lane £2 13s 4d; the same to the prior of Bermondsey (Burmundeseye) 9s 0d; the same to the prioress of Clerkenwell 9s 0d; the same to the minoresses outside Aldgate 5s 9d; the college of Kingston on Thames (Kynggeston) which Joan Wetherfeld holds £4 0s 0d; the same college which Richard Blounville holds £4 0s 0d; John Weston which William Kirkton holds to the prioress of Clerkenwell 3s 0d.

From the tenements of William Brampton to the church of St Paul 16s 0d.

426. From a tenement of John Elyngham which Richard Clement holds to the abbot of Chertsey (Chertesey) 5s 0d.

From a shop of the wardens of St Michael Crooked Lane which Robert Longe holds 10s 0d; from a brew house of the same wardens which John Burwell holds £2 0s 0d; from a shop of the same which John Whyte holds 10s 0d; from a tenement of the same which Nicholas Teperton holds £1 0s 0d.

From nine dwelling houses of the college of Kingston on Thames £4 10s 0d; from a large cellar of the same college which Maud Whiteheued holds £1 6s 8d.

From a tenement of: the wardens of St Michael which Richard Brandon holds £4 0s 0d; Henry Whitewelle to the prior of Bermondsey 6d; the abbot of St Mary Graces which Henry Prest holds £2 10s 0d.

From a messuage of the same abbot which Maud Whiteheuede holds £2 10s 0d.

427. PARISH OF ST MAGNUS THE MARTYR.

From a tenement of: John Bray which Hugh Gravele holds to the church of St Magnus £2 0s 0d; the wardens of the church of St Magnus which Richard Wynter holds £6 0s 0d; William Bys to the rector of the church of St Michael Crooked Lane £4 0s 0d; mr John Turk which Nicholas Aghton holds £6 6s 8d.

From the tenements of: Robert Rameseye to the prior of Southwark £2 6s 8d; Thomas Mockyng clerk to the church of St Magnus £1 6s 8d; item to the church of St Pancras 16s 0d; item to the abbot of Waltham 3s 0d; item to the church of St Helen 1s 0d.

From a tenement of William Hide which Richard Style holds to Southwark priory 16s 0d.

From a shop of Henry Hamond to the prior of Merton 10s 0d.

From three shops of Andrew Pyebakere to the nuns of St Helen £1 1s 0d.

From the church of St Magnus for an inn which Robert Ramseye has £6 13s 4d; to the hospital of St Giles from the same £1 6s 8d.

From the church of St Magnus for a shop of John Claidon £2 0s 0d.

428. From a shop of [blank] Somerville goldsmith to Southwark priory 15s 0d; from thence belonging to Westminster 2s 8d.[1]

From a tenement of: Angelus Christofre to the abbot of Westminster 3s 0d; the wardens of the church of St Magnus which Thomas Trugg and John York hold £3 0s 0d; the same wardens which Walter atte Welle holds £4 13s 4d; William Bys which John More holds to the church of St Michael Crooked Lane £1 6s 8d; the prioress of Dartford £10 0s 0d; Henry Yevele to John West chaplain £2 0s 0d.

From three tenements of the fraternity of Salve Regina £5 0s 0d.

From two tenements of Richard Cok £6 13s 4d.

From the tenements of the master of the college of Chaddesden £16 0s 0d.

From two tenements of the prior of Southwark £10 0s 0d.

From the tenements of William Radwell to the church of St Magnus £2 0s 0d.

From two tenements of the fraternity of Salve Regina in the church of St Magnus £6 0s 0d.

1. The taxation column has 2s 1d.

429. PARISH OF ST MARGARET FISH STREET HILL.

From an inn of Robert Ramseye esquire to the abbot of Westminster 8s 0d; item to the church of Holy Trinity the Less 13s 4d; item to Southwark priory 6s 8d.

From a shop of Gilbert Maghfield 13s 4d.

From a tenement of Thomas Morice to the prior of Bermondsey 12s 0d; item to Southwark priory 4s 0d; item to the church of St Margaret Fish Street Hill 10s 0d.

From the tenements of: the wardens of the church of St Magnus £4 0s 0d; Peter Grubbe to the hospital of St Giles 5s 0d; the prior and convent of Southwark £1 10s 0d; the prior of the Charterhouse £2 13s 4d; the same prior £1 0s 0d.

430. From a tenement of the rector and parishioners of St Margaret Fish Street Hill £2 0s 0d.

From the tenements of: Thomas Morice to the church of St Paul 1s 4d;[1] Thomas Palmere to the hospital of St Giles 10s 0d; Richard Radwelle to the prior of Bermondsey [blank]; the wife of Henry Cauntebrigge to the nuns of Haliwell £1 0s 0d; John Pays to Southwark priory 4s 0d; Thomas Morice to the prioress of Haliwell £1 0s 0d; the same to the abbot of Westminster 4s 6d; John Walleworthe for five candles in the church of St Margaret Fish Street Hill 5s 0d.

From a hospice with tenements of John Curteys to the abbot of Westminster £1 16s 10d; item to dame Joan Pentre nun of Halliwell £1 0s 0d; item from a cellar of the same John [sic] to the prior of the Charterhouse 13s 4d; item to the church of Holy Trinity the Less 3s 4d.

1. The taxation column has 2s 8d.

431. From the tenements of: the prior and convent of Christ Church Canterbury £10 0s 0d; John Walleworth vintner to the abbot of Westminster 4s 0d; Alice Doget to the abbot of St Mary Graces £3 6s 8d; Thomas Bakton to the house of Newark next Ripley (Rippele) 10s 0d; Stephen Derneford to Christ Church Canterbury 10d; item to the hospital of St Giles Holborn 1s 8d.

From the tenements of: the prioress of St Helen £8 13s 4d; the rector and parishioners of the church of St Leonard £2 13s 4d; the prior of Holy Trinity £5 0s 0d; the rectors and parishioners of St Leonard and of St Clement £1 10s 0d; John Bronnesbury to the rectors and parishioners of St Leonard and of St Clement £1 6s 8d; item to the abbot of Westminster 8s 0d; item to the prior of Southwark 8s 0d.

432. [m. 3d] From: one shop of the prior of Bermondsey £1 0s 0d; one tenement of John Brakynbergh to the house of Bermondsey 16s 0d; one inn which John Gillyng holds to the church of St Paul £2 13s 4d; the tenements which John Baldewell holds to the church of Holy Trinity 15s 2d.

Note. From the tenements of the prior of St Bartholomew £4 0s 0d.

From two shops which John holds to the house of Haliwell £2 0s 0d.

From a tenement of Richard Frank to the church of St Andrew Hubbard 1s 2d.

From two shops: of John Maldon to the said church of St Andrew 1s 2d; of the church of St Botolph £2 0s 0d.

From the tenements of: the rector and parishioners of St Leonard £2 13s 4d; John Pycard to the abbot of Westminster 14s 8d.

433. PARISH OF ST BENET GRACECHURCH.

Tenements of John Pountfreit or Pountfreyt: to the said church of St Benet £1 6s 8d; from another to the prioress of Clerkenwell £6 13s 4d; to the church of Holy Trinity [the Less] 13s 4d; from the same tenement to the abbot of Reading 4s 0d; to the abbot of Waltham £1 2s 6d.

From the tenements of: the prior of Merton £13 6s 8d; Richard Hatfeld to the abbey [sic] of Newark 7s 0d; item to the church of Holy Trinity 7s 0d; item to the master of the [New] Temple 3s 0d.

From the tenements of: London bridge which Richard Stotard holds to the abbot of St Mary Graces £3 6s 8d; William Olyver to the prior of Elsing Spital £1 0s 0d; Richard Spenser to the church of Holy Trinity

[the Less] £1 0s 0d; item to the hospital (church) of St Katherine by the Tower £1 2s 0d.
From the tenements of: the prior of Southwark £3 0s 0d; Thomas Wyght to the rector of St Mary at Hill £3 6s 8d.

£288 11s 11d.

434. CASTLE BAYNARD WARD.
From the tenements of: Ralph rector of the church of Widmerpool (Wygmorpoule) £2 0s 0d; John Chitterne in Peter's Lane (Peterlane) £10 0s 0d;[1] the Charterhouse £2 0s 0d; *Note* the house of St Bartholomew £9 5s 8d; the dean and chapter of St Paul £28 10s 8d; John Curtays to the same dean and chapter 10s 0d; Geoffrey Sutton to the same dean and chapter 16s 0d; Thomas Pynnore to the hospital of St Giles 4s 0d; John Boshome (?) to the same hospital 14s 0d; the same John to the hospital of St James £1 2s 0d; the earl of Salisbury to the dean and chapter of St Paul £1 10s 0d; from the same tenements to the abbot of Chertsey (Cherdeseye) £1 0s 0d *without*; item from the tenement which John Fraunkeleyn holds to the church of St Martin le Grand £2 13s 4d.
1. The first two entries are crossed through.

435. From the tenements of: the abbot of Fécamp (Fescaunpe) £3 6s 0d; the abbot and convent of Woburn £13 0s 0d; the hospital of St Mary without Bishopsgate which Richard Godard holds £3 6s 7d; the same hospital which Reginald Thorney holds £2 13s 4d; Elsing Spital which Richard Morys holds £8 0s 0d; Christine Sakevile to Reginald Spaldyng chaplain 11s 6d; John Reynald to the prior of Holy Trinity 6s 7d; from the same tenements to the prior and convent of Merton 4s 0d; Nicholas Taylour to the prior of St Bartholomew 10s 0d.
From a chantry which John West clerk has in the church of St Paul £6 0s 0d.
From the tenements in which Thomas de St Albans lives to the abbot of St Albans 10s 10d (?).
From the tenement which John Shakell holds to the abbot of Croxton £1 13s 4d.
From the tenements of: the church of St Martin le Grand £3 0s 0d (?); the church of St Paul on the south side of Sermon Lane (Sermonerslane) £2 5s 0d; the same on the north side £5 6s 8d; the said church of St Paul which Robert Halom holds £4 13s 4d; the prior and convent of Newark £4 0s 0d; the church of St Paul in which John Haddon lives £2 4s 0d; Adam Bamme to the nuns of Haliwell 9s 0d; William Acton to the nuns of Barking (Berkyng) 6s 8d; sir Hugh Wolf kt to the nuns of Clerkenwell and of Halliwell £2 10s 0d; John Trigge to the prior and convent of Merton £1 0s 0d; the church of St Paul which Michael Chut holds £2 10s 0d.

436. From the tenements of: the house of nuns of St Helen £5 0s 0d; the Friars Preachers of London at la Wharf £4 1s 4d; the prior of Bisham (Burstelesham) at la Wharf £9 0s 0d; the abbot of Barlings (Barlyng) £4 6s 8d; item to the hospital of St Bartholomew £1 0s 0d; *Note* Thomas

Freek to the same hospital £1 0s 0d; the abbot of Reading with wharves £20 6s 8d; Thomas Albon to the abbess of Burnham £2 0s 0d; John Asshebornham to the hospital of St Bartholomew 4s 0d; John Syferwas to the same hospital 4s 0d; Margaret Foxton to the church of St James Garlickhithe £2 10s 0d; from the same to the hospital of St Bartholomew 13s 0d.

From the tenements in which Thomas de St Albans lives to the abbot of St Albans 10s 0d.

From the tenements of: the abbot and convent of Croxton which John Shakell holds to the said abbot and convent £1 13s 4d; John Orwell servant at arms of the king to the church of St Thomas of Acon £1 6s 8d; item to the church of St Paul 13s 4d.

The house of Henry Ovyng to the bishop of London 13s 4d.

£166 0s 6d.

437. [m. 4] BASSISHAW WARD.
Prior of Elsing Spital. From the tenement which: Richard Oseberne holds £1 13s 4d; John Ram holds £1 4s 0d. From a shop which: Katherine Sprot holds 5s 0d; Isabel Hande holds 6s 0d; Roger Mathew holds 5s 0d; Thomas Yakeslee holds 6s 0d. From the rent of John Clerk poulterer £2 0s 0d.

Prioress of Clerkenwell. From the tenement which: Thomas Wyke holds 10s 0d; William Bronde holds 15s 0d. From the rent of William Hawe 4s 0d.

438. *Warden of Merton College Oxford (domus de Marton).* From a shop which: Isabel Kent holds 4s 0d; Thomas Horwode holds 4s 0d. Item: from another house there £2 10s 0d; from a shop which John Buckelsmyth holds 4s 0d; from the tenement of the prior of Southwark 15s 0d.

St Mary Magdalen Milk Street. From the house which: John Latonner holds 10s 0d; John Blaunche holds 10s 0d; Thomas Brewer holds 10s 0d. From a shop which: Lucy Baker holds 6s 0d; Margaret Hill holds 6s 0d. From a house which: Peter Morys holds £4 0s 0d; Alice Walden holds 8s 0d; Geoffrey Mason holds 13s 0d. From four houses which Thomas Beneyt holds £2 13s 4d.

439. *Rents of the prior of Holy Trinity.* From a tenement which: John Sandon holds 10s 0d; Richard Pelle holds £1 0s 0d. From a house which Robert Sothern holds £1 0s 0d. From a shop which John Carpenterre holds 8s 0d. From a house which John Somersford holds £3 6s 8d. From a shop which Margaret Wirdrawer holds 8s 0d. From a house 10s 0d; from another house 13s 4d. From a house which: Richard Plommer holds 16s 0d; William Lerpoll holds 12s 0d; Andrew Jordon holds 16s 0d.

440. *Dwelling-house (mansio) of the rector of Bassishaw.* From the dwelling house of the rector of St Michael Bassishaw £1 0s 0d.

Master of the house of St Thomas of Acon. From the tenement of Robert de Louthe £1 0s 0d.

Haliwell. From the tenement of John Davy 14s 0d.
Holy Trinity. From the tenement of John Davy 2s 0d.
Hospital of St Mary without Bishopsgate. From the rent of John Clerk poulterer 8s 0d.
Hospital of St James. From rent of: the same John Clerk 6s 8d; Agnes atte Hale £1 0s 0d.
Southwark priory. From rent of Simon Staundissh 2s 0d.
Church of St John Walbrook. From rent of the same Simon 6s 8d.
Holy Trinity. From rent of Henry Tamworth 15s 0d.

441. *Warden of Merton College.* From rents of lady Kiryell 14s 0d.
Haliwell. From rent of William Hawe 13s 0d.
Priory (church) of St Augustine Canterbury. From the tenements formerly of Richard Briggesworth £2 0s 0d.
Hospital of St James. From rent of Adam Fraunceys 17s 0d.
Hospital of St Bartholomew. From rent of the same Adam 5s 0d.
Prior of Holy Trinity. From rent of the same Adam 13s 4d.
Church of St Mary Aldermanbury. From rent of the same Adam 10s 0d.
A London rector for an allowance (person' London pour pitaunc'). From rent of the same Adam 10s 0d.

£42 18s 4d.

442. COLEMAN STREET WARD.
Master of [the hospital of St Thomas] of Acon. From the master £9 10s 8d.
Abbot of Waltham. From the tenement of sir Fitz Walter 4s 0d.
Master of [the hospital of] St Katherine. From the master £16 2s 0d.
Westminster. From the abbot 8s 0d. From the tenements of: Alice Marchaunt 3s 0d; Elias Fraunceys £1 0s 0d.
Prior of Holy Trinity. From the prior £6 0s 0d.
Church of [St Stephen] Coleman Street. From the tenements of the same prior 1s 0d.
John Kelyng chaplain. From the tenements of William Cressewyk and Richard Forster £2 6s 8d.
Clerkenwell. From the prioress £2 13s 4d.

443. *John Kelyng chaplain.* From the tenement of William Kyng 8s 0d.
Church of St Dionis [Backchurch]. From the church of St Dionis Graschirch £2 13s 4d.
Prior of St Bartholomew. From the same tenements 2s 0d.
John Kelyng chaplain. From the tenement of John Croydon 12s 0d.
Prior of St Bartholomew. From the same tenements 2s 0d.
Roger Horewode chaplain. From the same £4 0s 0d.
John Kelyng chaplain. From the tenements of: John Stondon £1 6s 8d; Robert Malpas 13s 4d.
Prior of St Bartholomew. From the tenements of John Lane 6s 0d.
Westminster. From the tenements of Edmund Hoddesdon 2s 0d.
Church of St Margaret Lothbury. From the tenements of the same Edmund 8s 0d.

Hospital of St Bartholomew. From the tenements of Thomas Boterwyk £1 0s 0d.

444. *Clerkenwell.* From the prioress £8 0s 0d.
Master of St Thomas of Acon. From the master £4 0s 0d.
Church of St Mary Bothaw (Botherhawe). From the same church £9 0s 0d; from the tenements of Paul Salesbery £4 0s 0d.
Prioress of Haliwell. From the tenement of Hugh Fastolf £1 0s 0d.
Abbot of Rewley (Regal' Loco). From the same abbot £24 0s 0d.
Roger Horwode chaplain. From the same £4 0s 0d.
Kelyng chaplain. From the tenement of John Bradeford chivaler £2 0s 0d.
Master of St Thomas of Acon. From the tenements of Simon Goldesburgh 6d.
[Illegible] of St Martin. From the tenements of the same Simon 6s 0d.
Prior of Elsing Spital. From the tenements of the same Simon 4s 0d.
Prior of the Charterhouse. From the same prior £12 13s 4d.

£119 5s 10d.

445. [m. 4d] QUEENHITHE WARD.
From the tenements of: William Wynter to Elsing Spital £3 6s 8d; Agnes Colkyn to Christ Church Canterbury 6s 3½d; item from the same to the prior of Elsing Spital 5s 0d; the abbot of Lesnes £6 13s 4d; William Olyver to Southwark priory £1 6s 8d; item to the church of St Paul 16s 0d; the church of St Paul in Timberhithe Lane (Tymbyrhithelane) £1 0s 0d; the same church £8 0s 0d; John Trigge and [blank] Lynchelade to the priory of Southwark [blank]; the prior of Newark £4 0s 0d; John Trigg for a chantry of John Bery £2 0s 0d; William Venour to the church of St Pancras 10s 0d; item from the same to the church of St Mary Somerset for a chantry £4 6s 8d.

446. From the tenements of: the rector of the church of St Mary Somerset £1 6s 8d; Adam Fraunceys to the same church 4s 0d; Adam Fraunceys to the abbot of Waltham £1 4s 0d; John Curuer [blank] of Clerkenwell 16s 0d; John Lyncoln [blank] of Clerkenwell 16s 0d; William Eynsham to Southwark priory 14s 0d; Stephen Spelman to the hospital of St Giles £2 0s 0d; the same Stephen [blank] of Clerkenwell 14s 0d; the former wife of John Setoun' to Southwark priory £5 8s 6d; Thomas Medlane to the hospital of St Thomas Southwark 7s 0d; John Gamboun to Bermondsey 12s 0d; the rector of the church of St Michael Crooked Lane £5 6s 8d; Robert Parys to Christ Church Canterbury 2s 6d; the prior of St John [Clerkenwell] £2 0s 0d; the abbot of Lesnes £6 11s 8d; the abbot of St Mary Graces £6 13s 4d.

447. Rents of a chantry of St Mildred Bread Street [blank]; item a tenement of the prior of Southwark 8s 0d.
From the tenements of: William Rykhill to the prior of Merton 14s 0d; John Vautort to the prior of Bermondsey 13s 4d; Joan who was the wife of William de Bury to the church of St Nicholas Cole Abbey 10s 0d; the

same Joan to the church of St Paul 13s 4d; from the same to Southwark priory 5s 0d.
From the tenement formerly of John Rothyng belonging to the church of St James Garlickhithe £6 0s 0d.
From the tenements of: the bishop of Winchester £5 0s 0d; Katherine Lokyn to the church of St Nicholas Cole Abbey 10s 0d; John Combe to the prior of Merton 5s 0d; the dean and chapter of St Paul £2 0s 0d; the abbot of Chertsey £3 0s 0d; William Kelsell to a certain chaplain for a certain chantry £4 6s 8d; the prioress of Newington (Novo Eton) £6 8s 0d.

448. From the tenements of: the earl of Stafford to the abbot of Sawtry £6 13s 4d; Avice Holweye to the same abbot £4 0s 0d; item to the prior of Bermondsey 12s 0d; the prior of Holy Trinity [blank]; sir Roger Holme £11 0s 0d; Ralph Double to the dean and chapter of St Paul 5s 0d; sir John Kyng chaplain to the church of St Paul [blank]; the same to sir William Ryffyn chaplain £1 13s 4d; John Graveneye to the prior of Bermondsey 10s 0d; item to the abbot of St Mary Graces 3s 4d; Richard Horwode to the church of St Nicholas Acon (Hacon) 2s 0d; Robert Risby to the church of St Antonin 13s 4d; Agnes Watlyngton to sir John Parker chaplain 13s 4d; William Olyver which he holds to certain priests £1 10s 0d.

£125 15s 10½d.

449. [m. 5] ALDGATE WARD.
House of St Katherine. From the tenements of Agnes atte Halle 2s 6d.
Hospital of St Thomas Southwark. From tenements of the same Agnes 3s 4d.
Prior of Holy Trinity. From tenements of the same Agnes 12s 0d.
Holy Trinity. From the tenements of: Thomas Coke 1s 0d; William atte Grove £3 6s 8d.
Hospital of St Thomas Southwark. From tenements of the same William 13s 4d.
Holy Trinity. From the tenement of John Rotour £2 0s 0d. Rents of the prior of Holy Trinity £77 15s 0d. From the tenement which: John Cosham holds £1 0s 0d; the same John holds 3s 0d.
Hornchurch. From another tenement which Richard Laugher holds £4 0s 0d.
Prior of Holy Trinity. From the tenement which: John Trigg holds £4 13s 4d; Thomas Porter holds £2 0s 0d.

450. *Prioress of Dartford.* Rents of the prioress £7 16s 0d.
Abbot of Evesham. Rents of the abbot £27 4s 0d.
Hospital of St Thomas Southwark. From the tenement of Adam Seton with nine shops 2s 6d.
Prior of Holy Trinity. From two shops with one upper room which John Sybil holds 3s 4d. From the tenement which Walter Waltham holds with two shops 6s 8d. From the tenements of Henry Parker with two shops 11s 0d.
Abbot of Bury [St Edmunds]. Rents of the abbot with five shops £10 0s 0d.

Haliwell. From the tenements of Agnes atte Hale 10s 0d.
Hospital of St Giles. From tenements of the same Agnes 4s 0d.
Barnwell (Bernewell). From tenements of the same Agnes 8s 4d.
Ramsey. From the same tenements 5s 0d.

451. *Abbot of Beeleigh (Byly).* Rents of the abbot £1 6s 8d. From the
tenements of John Donyngton 6s 8d.
House of Merton. From the same tenements 6s 8d.
Prior of Holy Trinity. Rents of the prior £2 3s 4d.
Holy Trinity. From the tenement of Thomas Eyston 12s 0d.
Church of St Augustine on the Wall. From the tenement of William Creswyk
3s 4d.
Bermondsey. From the tenement of Elias Thorp 10s 0d.
Elsing Spital. Rents of the prior £3 3s 4d.
Abbot of Lesnes. Rents of the abbot of Lesnes £11 18s 0d.
Southwark priory and St James (Seint Jakes). From the tenements of
Edmund Halstede £1 6s 8d.
St Lawrence Pountney. From the tenements of Thomas Broun £5 13s 4d.
St Martin le Grand. From the tenements of the same Thomas 13s 4d.
Holy Trinity. From the tenements of William Coggeshale £1 10s 8d.
House of St Helen. From the tenements of the same William 8s 0d.

452. *Holy Trinity.* From the tenements of: Thomas Otteley 8s 8d; Henry
atte Hoke 3s 4d. From seven shops of Richard Blumvill 4s 0d. From the
tenements of: lord de la Marche 5s 0d; sir Richard Scrope 6s 6d;
Richard Morell 3s 0d; John Bersaire £1 0s 0d; Reginald Burwell 8s 0d.
Church of St Olave. From the tenements of the said Reginald 5s 0d.
Holy Trinity. From the tenements of Thomas Mallyng £1 10s 0d.
Crutched friars. Rents of the friars £12 0s 4d.
Holy Trinity. From the tenements of John Normanton 1s 0d.
Hospital [sic] *of St Helen.* Rents of St Helen £2 0s 0d.
Hospital of St Mary. Rents of St Mary £6 5s 0d.
Holy Trinity. From the tenements of John de Gravesend 3s 0d.

£198 6s 8d.

453. BISHOPSGATE WARD (Bysshoppesgate).
Church of St Paul. From the tenements of Godfrey Cost £1 10s 0d.
Monastery [sic] *of Ely.* From tenements of the same Godfrey £1 10s 0d.
Haliwell. From tenements of the same Godfrey £1 6s 8d.
Holy Trinity. From the tenements of John Pykard 12s 0d.
[*All Hallows Lombard Street*] (*Graschirch*). From the tenements of Godfrey
Cost, Adam Rattesey, Richard Mildenhale and John Buke 4s 0d; from
the same tenements for the work of the same church 1s 0d.
From the same for the work of Christ Church Canterbury 2s 4d.
Rents of: the rector of the church of St Peter Cornhill £11 6s 8d; the same
rector viz. le Christophor £12 0s 0d.
Hospital of St Mary. From the tenements: which Thomas Brook tailor
holds £1 6s 8d; of Peter Danyell £1 12s 0d; of John atte Wode £1 0s 0d.

54

454. [*Illegible*] *Helen.* From the tenement of John Orgon 4s 8d.

Rector of St Peter Cornhill. From the rent which John Couper holds £1 6s 8d. From the tenements of: William Curtays £1 6s 8d; John Hamond £2 0s 0d. Item from two rents in a certain alley £1 6s 8d. From two shops which John Mogoun holds £1 14s 0d.

[*Illegible*]. From the tenements of Henry Duraunt 6s 8d.

Rector of the church of St Peter. Rent of sir John Mansyn called le Harne £6 13s 4d.

Hospital of St Bartholomew. From the rent of Adam Ramseye £1 10s 0d.

[*Illegible*] *Helen.* Rents of the prioress of St Helen £6 10s 0d.

Hospital of St Bartholomew. From the tenement of Ralph Hunte £1 10s 0d.

Westminster. From the tenement of John Bosham £1 0s 0d.

Hospital of St Giles. From the same tenements 6s 8d.

455. *Rents of St Helen.* Rents of: St Helen £104 4s 4d; the same prioress £9 12s 8d.

Church of St Martin Pomery. From the tenements of Maud Holbeche £4 16s 8d.

Prioress of St Helen. From the same tenements 15s 0d.

Abbey of Waltham. From the same tenements 4s 6d.

Rents of the prioress of St Helen £3 2s 8d.

Holy Trinity. From the tenements of William Brampton 10s 0d.

Prioress of St Helen. From the tenements of John Exsale 11s 8d.

[*St*] *Katherine.* From the same tenements 2s 0d.

[*Illegible*] *of St Thomas of Acon.* From the tenements of Adam Fraunceys 10s 0d.

Hospital of St Mary. From the tenements of Gilbert Meldeborne £1 10s 0d.

456. [m. 5d] BISHOPSGATE WARD Continued.

Church of St Paul. From the tenements of William Faryndon 7s 0d.

Church of St Botolph. From the tenements of the same William 4s 0d.

Abbey [*sic*] *of Dunmow.* From tenements of the same William 3s 0d.

Hospital of St Mary. From the rent of: John Norhampton £1 2s 0d; Andrew Tailliour 10s 0d; William Wandar(?) 12s 0d.

Bethlehem. Rents of the house of Bethlehem £2 0s 0d.

St James next Westminster. From the rent of Richard Loundres 4s 0d.

Hospital of St Mary. From the rent of John Wight 17s 0d. From the tenements of: Maud Bromholm 2s 0d; Richard Chandeler 16s 0d.

Master of St Thomas of Acon. From the tenements of Richard Hoke 10s 0d.

Southwark priory. From the tenements of the same Richard 4s 0d.

457. *Hospital of St Mary.* Rents of: a shop 12s 0d; another shop next door 13s 4d; William Mokeron £2 0s 0d.

Nuns of Stratford-at-Bow. From the rent of Margery Bone 8s 0d.

Hospital of St Mary. From two shops of Geoffrey Lethe £1 6s 8d. From the tenement of Henry Carpenter 9s 0d. Rents of: two shops £1 4s 0d; four shops of Walter Burgate £1 6s 8d; two shops 19s 0d.

[*St*] *Lawrence Pountney.* From the rent of Robert Estfeld 13s 4d. Rents £2 0s 0d.

458. *Hospital of St Mary.* Rents of the hospital from: ten shops £3 6s 8d; four shops £1 12s 0d; one messuage £1 8s 0d; six shops £3 0s 0d; seven shops £3 8s 0d. From the rent of Hornworth with a shop £2 5s 0d. From two shops 16s 0d; nine shops £2 5s 0d.

Crutched friars. From the rent which John Sperhunk holds £1 0s 0d.

Hospital of St Mary. From five shops £2 0s 0d.

Charterhouse. From the rent of Thomas Strode £1 10s 0d.

Bethlehem. Rents of Bethlehem with two shops £1 15s 0d.

Westminster. From the rent of Richard atte Stulpes 5s 0d.

Hospital of St Bartholomew. From the rent called le Dragon £1 16s 0d.

Holy Trinity. From the same rent 3s 0d.

459. *Prior of the hospital of St Mary.* From the tenements: of Nicholas Lyndon £2 0s 0d; of Thomas atte Swanne 10s 0d; outside the gate £1 13s 4d; of Henry Herbert £2 0s 0d; of John Gravysende £1 6s 8d; which the same John holds £2 0s 0d; of sir Simon [blank] £1 0s 0d; of Henry Herbery £3 0s 0d; of lady de Langford £3 0s 0d; of Thomas Gerbrigg £1 6s 8d; of Alice Ball £1 0s 0d; in the cemetery £1 0s 0d.

Dwelling-houses within the precinct of Bethlehem £2 0s 0d.

Nuns of St Helen. From the tenements of John Chircheman 6s 0d.

Holy Trinity. From the tenements of the same John 3s 0d.

Prior of Southwark. From the tenements of the same John 8s 8d.

Abbot of Reading. From the same tenements 2s 0d.

£152 12s 2d.

460. [m. 6] FARRINGDON WARD WITHIN.

Chantry. From the tenement of sir Nicholas chaplain of Aldermanbury £8 0s 0d.

Church of St Paul. From the tenements of sir Richard chaplain of the same church £3 18s 0d.

Abbot of Westminster. From the tenements of the abbot £1 13s 4d.

Prioress of St Helen. From a shop which John Somervyle holds £6 13s 4d.

Prior of Southwark. From a shop which Richard Broun holds £3 13s 4d.

Church of St Paul. From the tenements and shops of Drew Barantyn £6 0s 0d.

Prioress of Stratford-at-Bow. From the same tenements £3 0s 0d.

Abbot of Westminster. From three shops of Walter Strete 12s 0d.

Church of St Paul. From a shop of William Tyngewyk £2 0s 0d.

461. *Note. Hospital of St Bartholomew.* From shops of Henry Markeby 12s 0d.

Church of St Pancras. From the same shops 8s 0d.

Church of St Paul. From the tenement of Drew Barentyn 13s 0d.

Chantry. From the tenement of Peter Jay chaplain which Henry Grene holds £5 10s 0d.

Chapel of St Martin le Grand. From the tenements of John Kyng timber-monger £1 10s 0d.

Hospital of St Mary without Bishopsgate. From the same tenements £1 0s 0d.

Prioress of Haliwell. From the tenements of Thomas Polle 13s 4d.

Hospital of St Mary Bishopsgate. From the tenement which John Leyre holds 5s 0d.

Note. Prior of St Bartholomew. From the tenement of the prior which John Doncastre holds £11 0s 0d.

Chantry in 'le Peek'. From the tenements of Simon Doser and Henry Pomfreit £8 13s 4d.[1]

College of St Lawrence Pountney. From the tenement which Thomas Depham holds £10 0s 0d.

Church of St Paul. From the tenement which John Cantoys holds £12 6s 8d.

Elsing Spital. From the tenements of John Sechforde £6 13s 4d.

1. The taxation column has 18s 10½d.

462. *Church of St Paul.* From the tenement of John Sechforde 19s 4d.

Church of St Vedast. From the tenement of Roger Ryot £5 6s 8d.

Church of St Paul. From the tenement of John Carbonell 6s 6d.

Guildhall college. From its tenements £24 0s 0d.

Prioress of Clerkenwell. From the tenement of Bartholomew Castre 8s 0d.

Church of St Martin le Grand. From the tenement which Richard Saffrey holds £18 10s 0d.

Hospital of St Mary without Bishopsgate. From the tenement which Leonard Norton holds £6 13s 4d.

Abbot of St Mary Graces. From the tenement of the abbot and convent £2 13s 4d.

Prior of Merton. From the tenement of Richard Longe tailor 6s 0d.

Church of St Paul. From the tenement of Thomas Exton £1 10s 0d.

463. *Church of St Michael.* From the tenements which John Bowe spicer holds £1 0s 0d.

Church of St Vedast. From the same tenements £1 0s 0d.

Church of St Mary Staining. From the same tenements £1 0s 0d.

Church of St Paul. From the same tenements £1 16s 0d. From the tenements: of the dean and chapter £23 0s 0d; of sir Stephen chaplain £3 13s 4d; which John Cretyng holds £4 6s 8d.

Prior of Bermondsey. From the tenement of Thomas Wodehous 9s 0d.

Prioress of Cheshunt (Chesthonte). From the tenement of John Mokkyng 4s 0d.

Chantry. From the tenement of William Goldsmyth chaplain £5 0s 0d.

464. *Hospital of St Thomas Southwark.* From the tenement of Richard Russell 8s 0d.

Prioress of Cheshunt. From the tenement and shops of the prioress and convent £8 0s 0d.

Church of St Martin le Grand. From the tenement which John Trigg brewer holds £4 0s 0d.

Prior of Ely. From the tenement of the prior and chapter £12 10s 8d.

Dean of St Paul. From his tenement £11 0s 0d.

Bishop of London. From his tenement £26 6s 8d.

College of Chaddesden. From the tenement of the master and brothers £4 18s 8d.

Prioress of St Helen. From the tenement of the prioress and convent £2 6s 8d.

Church of St Paul. From the tenements of sirs: William de Colonia £5 6s 8d; Roger Holm £15 6s 8d; Ralph Wildebor £3 0s 0d; Roger Gerveys £2 0s 0d; Henry Assh £3 6s 8d.

465. *Prioress of Stratford-at-Bow.* From the tenement of the prioress and convent £3 9s 4d.

Chantry. From the tenement of William Ryffyn chaplain £4 0s 0d.

Church of St Paul. From the tenements of: the minor canons £5 0s 0d; sir Roger Holm £9 13s 4d.

Chantry. From the tenement of sir Laurence chaplain £10 0s 0d.

Friars preachers. From their tenement £5 3s 4d.

Prior of St Mary without Bishopsgate. From his tenement £1 6s 8d.

Abbot of Garendon (Garyndon). From his tenement £1 10s 0d.

Rents of the Charterhouse £3 0s 0d.

£331 8s 2d.

466. LANGBOURN WARD.

Rents of: *the hospital of St Mary without Bishopsgate* £4 8s 8d; *the abbot of St Mary Graces* £8 0s 0d; *the hospital* [sic] *of St Helen* £13 6s 8d; *the church of St Gabriel Fenchurch (Vanchirch)* £2 0s 0d; *the abbot of St Mary Graces* £6 0s 0d; *the church of St Benet Gracechurch* £6 13s 4d; mr John Turke £20 0s 0d; the [king's] chapel Westminster £4 0s 0d.

Chantry. Rents of sir William chaplain: which John Cloun holds £2 13s 4d; in St Clement's Lane £9 0s 0d.

Rents of: *the abbot of Stratford* in which Thomas Spenser patten-maker lives [blank]; *the vicarage of Fulham* £4 7s 4d; *the church of St Katherine* which Gautron de Bardes holds £8 0s 0d.

467. *Minoresses of Tower Hill.* From a tenement held by: John Meiz £1 6s 8d; William Colshull £1 6s 8d; Thomas Weston £1 6s 8d; Richard Taillour £1 6s 8d; Richard Kent cook 10s 0d; John Lorkyn £1 0s 0d; Richard Sadelere 16s 0d; John Lovekyn 9s 0d; Simon Feriby 10s 0d; Thomas Bernard 10s 0d; William Clerc 16s 0d; John Newman 16s 0d.

Church of St Mary Woolnoth. From a tenement held by: John Davy £1 6s 8d; John Barbour £1 6s 8d. From a messuage in 'Schetebournelane' £1 10s 0d.

House of St Helen. Rent of St Helen which Geoffrey Bristowe holds £1 6s 8d.

Prioress of Haliwell. From a tenement: in which no one lives 16s 0d; which Edmund Bury holds 12s 0d;[1] which John Prior holds 10s 0d.

1. The taxation column has 2s 8d.

468. [m. 6d] *Prioress of Clerkenwell.* From rent which David Dromy holds £6 0s 0d.

Abbey of Stratford. From the rent which Perot Baudy holds £10 0s 0d.

House of St Katherine. From the rent of Richard Bemoy 6s 0d.
Hospital of St Mary without Bishopsgate. Rent 12s 0d.
House of St Helen. From the same rent 3s 4d.
Hospital of St Thomas Southwark. From the same rent 3s 4d; from the
same rent 3s 4d.
Prior of Holy Trinity. From the rent of Ralph Parles 3s 4d.
House of St Katherine. From the same rent 5s 0d.
Church of [*St Mary*] *Staining.* From rent of the abbot of St Mary Graces
£8 0s 0d.
House of St Helen. From the rent of Philip Burton £3 0s 0d.
Prioress of Haliwell. From the rent of sir Robert Denny kt 12s 0d.
Church of St Gabriel Fenchurch (Vancherche). From rent of sir John Fysi-
mond 2s 0d.

469. *Church of Holy Trinity.* From rent of: John Emond 5s 0d; Thomas
Bole ironmonger 1s 8d; Roger Moigne draper 'A' 1s 8d; the rector of
the church of St Gabriel Fenchurch 13s 4d. From the same rent 1s 8d.
Haliwell. From the rent of John Warner 1s 0d.
Prior [*sic*] *of Kilburn.* From the rent of Thomas Aschhirst 4d.
Clerkenwell. From the rent of Thomas Bonauntr' 6s 8d.
Prior of St Bartholomew. From the rent of John Dyk 3s 4d.
Church of St Dionis (*Divonisii*). From the rent of Walter White 1s 0d.
Prioress of Kilburn. From the rent of Robert Cupgate 1s 0d.
Prior of Holy Trinity. From the rent of Adam Bamme 6s 8d.
Prior of Merton. From the rent of: Andrew Silkiston 1s 0d; John Capell
1s 8d.

470. *House of St Helen.* From the rent of John Langhorn 6s 0d.
Oxford college. From the rent of: the church of St Benet 10s 0d; Richard
Curteis 10s 0d.
Church of St Paul. From the rent of Benedict Cornewaill £1 0s 0d.[1]
From the rent of Ralph Parles to: *the house of St Helen* 2s 0d; *the abbot of
St Mary Graces* 2s 0d; *the abbot of Westminster* 1s 0d; *Bermondsey* 1s 0d;
the prior of Merton 3s 6d.
Prior of Ware. From the rent of Simon de Borw £2 0s 0d.
Holy Trinity. From the rent of Robert Wertele 3s 4d.
Church of St Paul. From the rent of: Adam Bamme 10s 0d; Godfrey Cost
£3 0s 0d.

1. The taxation column has 1s 8d.

471. *Abbot of St Mary Graces.* From the rent of John Turke £3 6s 8d.
Holy Trinity. From the rent of [the king's] chapel Westminster 3s 4d.
Chantry of St Edmund. From the rent of: John Chaundeleir £6 13s 4d; the
same 8s 8d.
Chantry of St Clement. From the rent of: the wife of Thomas Austyn
£4 0s 0d; sir William £9 0s 0d; the same 2s 0d.
Rector of St Clement. From the same rent 5s 0d.
Abbot of Stratford. From the rent of the vicarage of Fulham £1 0s 0d.
Church of St Paul. From the rent of Alice Pondre £1 0s 0d.

Holy Trinity. From the same rent 1s 0d.

472. From the rent of John Welbourne to: *Haliwell* 12s 0d; *Holy Trinity* 6s 8d; *the same* 3s 4d.
Rector of St Edmund. From rent of the college of Shottesbrooke (Schote-brok) 13s 4d.
Haliwell. From the rent of John Pays £3 0s 0d.[1]
Holy Trinity. From the rent of lady Alice Leycestre 5s 0d.
Church of St Clement. From the rent of: John Aspeland 2s 0d; Thomas Godlak does not pay 'A' 13s 0d.
Church of St Nicholas Acon. From the same rent 3s 0d.
Church of St Lawrence. From the same rent 11s 0d.
Church of St Nicholas Acon. From the rent of John Bereham 1s 0d.
Church of St Leonard Foster Lane (Fasterlane). From the rent of Thomas Moraunt £3 16s 8d.
Church of St Nicholas Acon. From the same rent 4s 0d.
Haliwell. From the rent of Adam Craft £1 4s 0d.
Church of St Nicholas Acon. From the same rent 6s 0d. From the rent of John Leycestre 2s 3d.
Church of St Nicholas. From the rent of John Wakele 5s 0d.

   1. The taxation column has £10 0s 0d.

473. *Faversham.* From the rent of [blank] de Lovyngton draper 2s 0d.
Reigate (Reygate). From the same rent 2s 0d.
Minoresses by the Tower. From the rent of sir William Pecche kt £8 0s 0d.
From the rent of Nicholas Hotot to: *the hospital of St Mary* 8s 0d; *Haliwell* 2s 0d; *the house of St Katherine* 2s 0d; *the hospital of St James* 2s 0d; *the same* paid 'A' 2s 0d.
Clerkenwell. From rent of the prioress £6 0s 0d.
Abbot of Stratford. From the rent of: Thomas Noket paid 'A' 2d;[1] the abbot £10 0s 0d.
£212 2s 11d.

   1. The taxation column has 4d.

474. [m. 7] ALDERSGATE WARD WITHIN (Aldrichesgate).
To the dean and chapter of the church of St Martin le Grand. From a tene-ment: in which the rector of [the church of] All Hallows Bread Street lives £2 13s 4d; of the dean and chapter £2 13s 4d; the same £2 6s 8d; of the dean which John Burton formerly held £4 0s 0d; of the dean which William Spaldewyk holds £2 13s 4d; of the dean and chapter which John Burbach holds £3 6s 8d.

475. From a tenement: of the abbot [sic] of Holy Trinity by the Tower which Walter Hoper holds £10 0s 0d; belonging to a certain chantry in the church of St Paul which John Parys holds £5 6s 8d; of the same church which John Luton holds £3 0s 0d; of the same church which Richard Fraunceys holds £2 0s 0d; of John de Bury to the hospital of St Mary without Bishopsgate 6s 8d; *without* of Thomas Welforde to the prior of St John of Jerusalem in England £1 6s 8d; of Thomas Hayz to the dean of St Martin 13s 4d; of John Bontyng to the prior of the hospital of St Mary without Bishopsgate 4s 0d; of the abbot of Westminster which mr Thomas Stowe holds £8 0s 0d; of John Knotte fishmonger to the prior of St Bartholomew 10s 0d, and to the abbot of Westminster 9s 0d, item to the parish church 3s 4d.

476. From a tenement: belonging to a certain nun of St Helen 16s 0d; of St Martin called Baudesrente £17 0s 0d;[1] *note* of the prior of St Bartholomew £2 0s 0d; of Thomas de St Albans to the prioress of Clerkenwell 13s 4d; of the rector of the church of St Vedast 10s 0d; of Robert Pelhill to the church of St Anne [and St Agnes] 3s 8d;[2] of the abbot of Warden £10 0s 0d; of the prior of Rochester £5 0s 0d; of John Frensshe to the same prior 14s 0d; of the London goldsmiths to the abbot of Woburn (Wowborne) 13s 4d; of Drew Barentyen to the abbot of St Albans 4s 0d; from the same tenement to the hospital of St James 3s 4d. Item: to the dean of St Martin le Grand 6s 8d; to the abbot of Westminster 13s 4d; *note* to the prior and convent of St Bartholomew £1 10s 0d; *note* to the hospital of St Bartholomew 13s 4d.

1. The taxation column has 8s 10d.
2. The taxation column has 3s 1d.

477. ALDERSGATE WARD WITHOUT.
From the tenement of the wife of Clement Spray to the hospital of St Giles 3s 4d. Item: to the abbot of Kirkstead (Kirkstede) £3 0s 0d; to the hospital of St John 11s 0d; to the prior of Southwark 3s 2d; to the hospital of St James 4s 0d.
Rents to the prior of Ogbourne £6 7s 8d.
From the tenement of Henry Hamwode to the hospital of St Bartholomew 17s 0d; item from the tenement of the same Henry to the prior of St Bartholomew 1s 8d.
From the tenement of: the rector of the church of St Botolph £9 0s 0d; William Stonham to the hospital of St Bartholomew £1 6s 8d; John Canynges to the same £1 0s 0d.
Note. Rents of: the prior of St Bartholomew £17 18s 8d; the abbot of Kirkstead (Kyrkestede) £1 0s 0d.

478. From the tenements of: Margaret Naples to the prior of St Bartholomew £2 13s 4d; *without* the wife of John Piel to the same prior £1 12s 0d; Philip atte Vyne to the same prior 8s 0d; from the same tenement to the hospital of St James 12s 0d; from the same tenement to the church of St Botolph 4s 0d; John Staunton to the prior of St Bartholomew 3s 0d; John Herteshorn to the prior of Hounslow (Hundeslowe) £1 12s 0d; sir Ralph Kasteyn to the prior of St Bartholomew 1s 6d; Thomas Willesdon to the same prior 2s 6d; from thence to the same prior 2s 6d;[1] from the tenement of the same Thomas to the prior of Hounslow £1 2s 0d; Alice Colwelle to the prior of St Bartholomew 4s 0d; Adam Bret to the same prior 14s 8d.

1. This item is crossed through.

479. Rents of the prior of the Charterhouse £16 7s 4d.

From the tenements of: William Clophill to the prior of St Bartholomew 3s 4d; William Cresewyk to the hospital of St Bartholomew 3s 4d.

The college of St Martin £1 0s 0d.

From the tenement of William Pounfrett to the church of St Botolph 1s 0d.

Rents of: the prior of Barnwell (Bernewelle) £6 0s 0d; the abbot of Walden £12 0s 0d; the almoner of St Paul £2 6s 8d.

From the tenements of: John Appilton to the hospital of St Bartholomew 15s 0d; John Bradmour to the church of St Paul 1s 6d.

£184 12s 2d. [Total for the whole ward.]

480. VINTRY WARD.

From the tenement which: the earl marshal holds to the [king's] chapel Westminster £13 6s 8d; John Marchal holds to the abbot of Rewley £20 0s 0d; Gilbert Bonet holds to the prioress of Kilburn £4 13s 4d; Richard Coleigne holds to the prior of Holy Trinity 3s 4d; William Rede holds to the rector of [the church of] St Thomas the Apostle £8 13s 4d.

Rents of: the church of St Lawrence Pountney which John Roket holds £10 16s 8d; the church of [St Mary] Aldermary which John Stapilton holds £5 0s 0d.

From the tenement which: Robert Marny holds to a chantry of [St Michael] Paternoster £4 13s 4d; Henry Herbury holds to the nuns of Cheshunt £3 13s 4d; Geoffrey Coupe holds to the prioress of St Helen £3 6s 8d; [blank] Mundene holds to the hospital of St Mary without Bishopsgate £3 3s 4d; Richard Lyttelyngton holds to the church of St Paul £1 6s 8d.

481. From the tenement which: Gilbert Merch' holds to the prior of Holy Trinity 5s 0d; William More holds to the hospital of St Mary without Bishopsgate £14 13s 4d; Thomas Lamyer holds to the abbot of St Mary Graces £3 6s 8d; [blank] Clovyle holds to the prior of Merton £1 0s 0d; John Cornwaleys holds to the chantry of [blank] Jesore £5 0s 0d; the same John holds to the abbot of Westminster 12s 0d; Henry Vannere holds to the hospital of St Bartholomew £10 13s 4d; Adam Vullere holds to the prior of St John of Jerusalem £9 2s 0d.

Rents of the rector of the church of St John Walbrook (Horshobrigge) £2 0s 0d.

The tenement which William Gavtron holds to the prior of Southwark £1 0s 0d.

Rents of the prior of St Bartholomew £23 10s 0d.

From the tenement which: Thomas Medelane holds to the hospital of St Giles £1 0s 0d; the same Thomas holds to the abbot of Westminster 6s 0d.

£151 5s 0d.

482. [m. 7d] LIME STREET WARD (Lymstret).

From the tenement of: Robert Denny to the nuns of Stratford-at-Bow 6s 0d; William Budby to the hospital of St Bartholomew 13s 4d; John Wyte maltmonger to the nuns of Stratford-at-Bow 4s 0d; Alice Preston to the church of St Helen 3s 0d; item to Clerkenwell 5s 0d; Ed' Fysymond to

the church of Holy Trinity [the Less] (the church of Christ) 4s 0d.
Rents of: the abbot of St Mary Graces £3 6s 8d; the prioress of St Helen
£16 0s 0d.
Brother Thomas of the Charterhouse £1 0s 0d.

£22 2s 0d.

483. CORNHILL WARD.
Rents of: the bishop of London £2 0s 0d; the rector of [the church of] St
Peter £4 0s 0d.
Church of St Peter Cornhill. From the tenements of Adam Lyoun 13s 4d.
Church of St Botolph. From the tenements of the same Adam atte Lyon
£1 0s 0d.
Church of St Martin le Grand. From the same tenements 6s 8d.
Prioress of Kilburn. From the same tenements 3s 4d.
Rents of the prioress of St Helen in which John Somersham lives £7 0s 0d.
Church of St Michael Cornhill. From the tenements of John Knyvesworth
1s 0d.
Church of St Pancras. From the same tenements 13s 4d.
Church of St Michael Cornhill. From the tenements of Andrew Smyth
£3 6s 8d.

484. Rents of: St Helen which John Northfolke holds £8 13s 4d; the college
of Sudbury £8 13s 4d; the hospital of St Thomas Southwark £11 0s 0d;
the college of Shottesbrooke (Shotisbrok) £12 0s 0d; Mokkyng clerk
£10 13s 4d.
Church of St Michael. From the tenements of: John Derlyng 9s 8d; the
same £1 3s 4d; the same 10s 0d; John Glenaunt £4 0s 0d.
New Temple. From the tenements of the same John 6s 0d.

485. Rents of: the prior of St Bartholomew £6 6s 8d; the hospital of St
Mary which Thomas Swanne holds £13 0s 0d.
Church of St Mary Woolnoth. From the tenements of Thomas Pyctotte 6s 8d.
Rents of mr Richard Boteller £6 13s 4d.
[St] *Michael Cornhill.* From the tenements of Thomas Irlound £3 6s 8d.
Holy Trinity. From the same tenements 3s 4d; from the tenements of
Thomas Wodehouse 3s 4d.
Rent of the Charterhouse which: Pykenham holds £5 6s 8d; Walter Fermour
holds £4 0s 0d; John Barre holds £2 0s 0d.

486. *Abbot of St Mary Graces.* From the tenements of Stephen Godewyn
£4 0s 0d.
Bermondsey (Bermundeshey). From the tenements of: Richard Willeston
3s 0d; Benedict Cornwayll 3s 0d.
Rector of St Christopher. From the tenements of: Richard Cheryngton
£1 17s 0d; John Sibill £3 9s 2d; John Claveryng £2 5s 4d.
Rent of Holy Trinity which Richard Wallden holds £5 6s 8d.
[St] *Mary Woolchurch.* From the tenements of: John Wallcotte 8s 0d; the
same £6 13s 4d.

487. [*St*] *Christopher*. From the tenements of John Walcotte £5 13s 4d.

Holy Trinity. From the tenements of Henry Caumbrygge 16s 0d. Rents of the prior £8 0s 0d.

Church of St Michael Cornhill. From the tenements of Agnes Leueysham £1 14s 0d.

Church of St Christopher. From the tenements of: John Hanham £3 6s 8d; John Got £3 6s 8d.

From the tenements of John Parker chaplain £10 13s 4d.

From the tenements of Katherine Lowkyn to: *the prior of St Bartholomew* 13s 0d; *the house of St Albans* 6s 0d; *the house of St Katherine* 5s 0d.

488. From the tenements of Richard Blumvill to: *the house of St Bartholomew* 13s 4d; *Clerkenwell* 13s 4d; *St Michael Cornhill* £7 0s 0d.

Church of St Benet. From the tenements of William Creswyk 'ii torches p's'.

Priory of St Helen. From tenements which John Gofair holds of the prioress £10 0s 0d.

Rent of St Michael Cornhill which John Muster holds £9 6s 8d.

A certain chantry in the county of York. From tenements of Edmund Sanford esquire £10 0s 0d.

Rents of the hospital of St Mary £10 0s 0d.

£222 16s 6d.

489. [m. 8] BREAD STREET WARD.

From the abbot of Westminster for the tenement of: John Frensshe which Thomas Bokyll holds 15s 0d; the same John which Thomas Polle and William Maryner hold 15s 0d.

From the tenement of the prior of Newark which Thomas Hay and the church of All Hallows hold £7 0s 0d.

From the prior of Bermondsey for the tenement of Robert Busse brazier which Adam Merifeld holds £1 0s 0d.

From the prioress of Haliwell for the tenement of Adam Merifeld and Thomas Exton which John Hunte holds £3 3s 4d.

Note. From the hospital of St Bartholomew for the tenement of lady Avice Tonge which John Wakelee holds £1 0s 0d.

From the prior of Holy Trinity for the tenement which John Grenefeld holds £1 6s 8d.

490. IN THE PARISH OF ST MARY MAGDALENE.

From the tenement of the master of St James which: Richard Lambert holds £2 0s 0d; Thomas Kirton haberdasher holds £2 0s 0d; Thomas Blakestok holds £1 16s 8d.

From the abbot of Westminster for the tenement of Hugh Lynne kt and Margery his wife which William Foucher holds £1 0s 0d. For the same from: the prior of Southwark £1 0s 0d; the house of St Helen £1 16s 0d;[1] the house of St James £4 12s 8d.

From the tenement of the master of St James: [blank]; which the wife of Henry Cornwaille holds £4 16s 8d.

From the Domus Conversorum (Convershall) for the tenement of Adam Frounceys kt which Thomas Fulbourne holds £1 0s 0d.

From the abbot of Westminster for shops of the same Adam next the house of the same Thomas and a tenement of the same Adam over the house of Fulbourne 13s 4d.

From the master of St James for the tenement of: William Pateney chaplain which John Raynald holds 10s 0d; Henry Frowyk which John Reynald holds and the tenement of William Burden which the same John holds 10s 0d.

1. The taxation column has 3s 0d.

491. IN THE PARISH OF ALL HALLOWS BREAD STREET.

From the master of St James for the tenement of John Forester £2 10s 0d; from the house of St Helen for the same £1 16s 0d.

From the master of St James for the tenement of sir Robert Denny kt which William Jurdan holds £2 10s 0d. From the tenement of the same master: which Robert Merston holds £4 0s 0d; which William Stapultee holds £4 0s 0d.

From the prioress of Haliwell for the tenement of Bartholomew Castre which John Wytleseye holds 13s 4d; to the hospital of St Mary without Bishopsgate for the same 13s 4d; to the prioress of Kilburn for the same 6s 8d.

From the prioress of Kilburn for the tenement of John Ayre 6s 8d.

Note. From the prior of St Bartholomew for the tenement of Thomas Botiller which John Kent innkeeper holds £1 0s 0d.

From the church of All Hallows from the tenement of John Sely which Hugh Corbrigg holds £3 6s 8d; from the prior of St Bartholomew for the same tenement 10s 0d; from the master of St Thomas of Acon for the same 8s 0d.

492. From the tenement of the prior of St Bartholomew which Thomas Colman holds £3 6s 8d.

From the archbishop of Canterbury for the tenements of William Baret £2 2s 0d; from the church of All Hallows for the same 6s 8d.

From the church of [St Mary] Aldermary for the tenement of Roger Parys 13s 4d.

Note. From the tenement of the prior of St Bartholomew £15 6s 8d.

From the abbot of Westminster for the tenement of Thomas Charleton which Richard Broun holds 6s 8d.

From the church of St Mildred for the tenements of sir John Montacu which John Walpolle holds £1 3s 2d; from the nuns of Clerkenwell for the same 13s 4d; item to the abbot of Westminster 1s 3d.

From the master of the hospital of St Giles for the tenement of Roger Parys which John Corner holds 8s 0d.

From the prior of Leeds (Ledes) for the tenement of Adam atte Water 10s 0d.

From John Burton clerk of the rolls for the tenement of John Shilyngford £2 0s 0d; item to the church of All Hallows £2 0s 0d.

493. From the Domus Conversorum for the tenements of Roger Parys and John Shilingford £1 11s 0d.

Note. From the master of the hospital of St Bartholomew for the tenement of Agnes atte Hale £2 5s 0d; item to the church of All Hallows 6s 8d; item to the archbishop of Canterbury 2s 0d.

From the monastery [sic] of St Paul for the tenement of John Wakelee 10s 0d.

From the tenement of the master [sic] of Merton college Oxford which William Popilton holds £4 6s 8d.

From sir Geoffrey canon of the church of St Paul for the tenement of the fraternity of the London goldsmiths £2 6s 8d; item to the almoner of St Paul £1 6s 8d; item to the dean of St Paul £1 6s 8d; item to the prioress of Kilburn 13s 4d.

£10 4s 11½d.

494. IN THE PARISH OF ST MILDRED.

From the church of St Mildred: for the tenement of Maud Penne 2s 4d; from rent called Wandeneshous £3 0s 8d.

From the prior of Holy Trinity for rents of Arnald Pynkeneye and Robert Langhorne 13s 4d.

From the hospital of St Giles for the tenement of Gilbert Baker 5s 9d; item from the dean of St Paul 4s 0d.

From the master of the hospital of St Giles from the tenement of William Shiryngham 13s 4d.

From the tenement of the church of St Margaret £1 16s 0d.

From the church of St Paul for the rent of John Redyng 4s 0d.

From the prior of Holy Trinity for the tenement of William Rason 4s 0d.

From the church of St Mildred for the tenement of John Clerk £1 2s 6d.

From the prior of Bermondsey for the tenement of Robert Chircheman 4s 0d.

From the prior of St John for the tenement of Paul Cisors £1 13s 4d.

From the prioress of Stratford-at-Bow for the tenement of Ralph Rede £2 0s 0d.

From the abbot of Westminster for the tenement of John Bray 3s 4d.

Rent of the abbot of Notley £14 0s 0d.

495. IN THE PARISH OF ST NICHOLAS COLE ABBEY.

From the tenements of: the church of St Paul which Richard Incliton holds £2 0s 0d; the prior of Newark which Robert Ragenhill holds £1 10s 0d.

From the hospital of St Giles for the shop of Richard Giffard 7s 0d; to the church of St Paul for the same 2s 0d.

From the prior of Holy Trinity for a tenement of William Tripe 7s 0d; *note* from the prior of St Bartholomew for a tenement with shop of the same 1s 9d; from the prioress of Haliwell for a shop of the same 2s 6d.

From the prior of Bermondsey for a tenement of John Ragenhill 12s 0d.

From the tenements of: the abbot of Biddlesden (Bitlesden) £1 6s 8d; the dean of St Martin[le Grand] £11 6s 8d.

From the abbot of Waltham for the tenement of Denys Lopham 13s 4d.

From the hospital of St Giles for the tenement of John Pilot 9s 0d.

From the tenement of the hospital of St Mary without Bishopsgate which Robert Crowmer holds £1 13s 4d.

£3 8s 4d. [In the taxation column].

496. [m. 8d] From the master of St James next Westminster from a shop on
the east side which John Ragenhill has 6s 0d; from the abbot of St Albans
for another shop of the same John 5s 0d; from the church of St
Nicholas Cole Abbey for the same 8s 0d.
From the abbot of Westminster for the tenement of John Blakeneye 10s 0d.
Tenement of the hospital [blank].
From the tenement of sir William Bridbroke rector of the same church of
St Nicholas £6 0s 0d; from thence to the hospital of St Bartholomew
£1 6s 8d.

497. PARISH OF ST AUGUSTINE.
From the church of St Audoen for rents of lord le Spencer £1 0s 0d; from
the prior of Newark for the same 5s 0d; from the church of St Paul for
the same 3s 4d.
Note. From the tenements of: the master of the hospital of St Bartholomew
£15 0s 0d; the rector of the church of St Vedast £21 13s 4d; mr William
Chambre for quit rent going to the master of St Giles 2s 0d; sir Richard
chaplain of a chantry of St Paul £5 14s 8d.
From the hospital of St James for the tenement of Robert York 6s 8d.
From the church of St Michael Crooked Lane for the tenement of William
Wyght £2 0s 0d.
From the nuns of Cheshunt for the tenement of Robert Chircheman 10s 0d.

£9 9s 2½d. [In the taxation column in another hand].

498. PARISH OF ST MARGARET MOSES [FRIDAY STEET].
From the church of St Margaret for the tenement of Thomas Bygood 6s 8d;
from the church of St Martin le Grand for the same 13s 4d.
From the prior of Bermondsey for the tenement of Roger Payn 10s 0d.
From the church of St Paul for the tenement of John Goldryng 6s 0d.
Note. From the hospital of St Bartholomew for the tenement of Roger
Parys £2 8s 0d.
From rents of: the abbot and convent of St Mary Graces £15 14s 8d; the
hospital of St Mary without Bishopsgate £2 13s 4d.
From the hospital of St Mary for the rent of Gilbert Baker £2 13s 4d.

£4 3s 10d. [In the taxation column].

499. PARISH OF ST JOHN THE EVANGELIST.
From the abbot of Westminster for the tenement of Richard Knowesle
£1 5s 0d; item from sir John Burton clerk of the rolls of chancery
£5 6s 8d.
From the tenements of St Paul which: Michael Cornwaill holds £7 2s 8d;
[blank] Grafton holds £2 10s 0d.
From the tenement of the rector of the church of St John: which Clifton
holds £2 0s 0d; which Robert York holds £1 4s 0d; viz. two small rooms
at the top of a staircase 12s 0d.

£3 7s 9d. [In the taxation column].

500. PARISH OF ST MATTHEW.
From the prior of St Gregory Canterbury for the tenement of Thomas
Wyght £2 0s 0d.
From the abbot of Westminster for the tenement of sir John Chambre
£1 0s 0d.

10s 0d. [In the taxation column].
rol' (?)

501. CANDLEWICK STREET WARD.

[The material listed here consists almost entirely of items which have appeared above.]

[**405** items 1–3]

St Clement.
A guildhall (guyhalde) chantry has rent from a tenement called le Cok on
the Hoop £6 13s 4d.[1]

[**407** items 1–2; **408** items 1–8; **409** items 1–3]

The church of St Martin Orgar has rent p.a. £3 6s 8d.

[**410** in full]

The prior of Hitchin has from rent in which Reginald Grille lives £8 0s 0d.

1. The taxation column is blank.

502. [m. 9] TOWER WARD.
From the tenements of: Geoffrey Maunfeld to *the abbess of Barking* 12s 0d
the same Geoffrey to *the prioress of Kilburn* 10s 0d; Adam Bamme to *the
abbot of St Mary Graces* £3 6s 8d; Thomas Pole to *Bermondsey* 17s 0d;
the same to *the hospital of St Bartholomew* 6s 8d; John Bedyng to *St
Edmund* [*King and Martyr*] (*Lumbardstret*) £1 6s 8d; Edmund Halstede
to *Westminster* £1 0s 0d; the same 6 [sic] to *Southwark priory* 6s 8d.
Rent of the abbot of Evesham (Evysham) £15 0s 0d.

503. From the tenements of: Richard Willesdonn to *the church of St Helen*
10s 0d; the same to *Southwark priory* 13s 4d; Hugh Falstolf to *Bermondsey* £1 0s 0d; the same to *Westminster* 6s 8d; lady Joan Vanner to *the
abbot of St Mary Graces* £3 6s 8d; Henry Irtoun to *Bermondsey* 8s 6d;
the same to *the hospital of St Mary* 8s 0d; Richard Brankweyn to *St
Martin le Grand* £2 13s 4d; the same Richard to *the hospital of St Mary*
£1 0s 0d; John Mountague to *Westminster* 5s 0d.

504. From the tenements of: Thomas Ally to *the abbot of Waltham* 6s 8d;
the same to *the hospital of St Mary* 4s 0d; Nicholas Potyn to *Holy
Trinity* 10s 0d; Thomas Broune to *the abbot of St Augustine* £1 0s 0d;
the same to *the prior of St Bartholomew* £1 4s 0d; sir Nicholas Dabris-
court to *Bermondsey* (*Barmundeshey*) 13s 4d; the same to *the church of
St Katherine* £1 0s 0d. Item from the tenements of lord de Grey to *Holy
Trinity* 5s 8d.
Rents of: the church of St Peter Paul's Wharf (Lamberdeshill) £1 13s 4d;
the abbot of Colchester (Colechestre) £5 0s 0d.

68

505. From the tenements of: John Heend to *Westminster* 3s 0d; the same to *Southwark priory* 7s 0d; John Gamell to *Holy Trinity* 6s 0d.
Rents of: the church of St Dunstan £2 13s 4d; the abbot of St Mary Graces £3 10s 0d; the crutched friars £8 0s 0d.
From the tenements of: Philip Burton to *Holy Trinity* 5s 0d; William Barett to *Kilburn* 12s 0d; Adam Fraunceys to *Barking* 13s 4d.
Rents of Richard Maykyng chaplain £7 0s 0d.

506. *Barking (Birrkyngchirch).* Rents of Robert chaplain £8 0s 0d.
Barking (Barkyngchirch). From rent of John Normanton 5s 0d.
Hospital of St Mary. From tenements of John Assheburne 6s 8d.
Clerkenwell. From tenements of Richard Turk 2s 0d.
Rents of the subprioress of Clerkenwell £1 0s 0d.
From the tenements of: William Assheforde to *the abbess of Barking* 1s 4d; [blank] Codyngton to *the church of St Katherine* 6s 0d; John FitzSimon chivaler to *Westminster* 2s 6d.
Rents of the church of St Dunstan in Mart Lane £4 0s 0d.
Holy Trinity. From the tenements of Robert Knolles chivaler 5s 0d.

507. Rents of: the crutched friars £6 0s 0d; the hospital of St Mary in Seething Lane (Sevedenlane) £2 0s 0d; the church of St Paul in Seething Lane (Sethedenlane) £6 0s 0d.
Abbot of Waltham. From the rents of Hugh Clerk 15s 0d.
Holy Trinity. From the same rents 2s 0d.
Master of St James. From the tenements of William Venour 1s 4d.
Rents of: the abbot of St Mary Graces £2 0s 0d; the crutched friars for two shops £1 0s 0d; the church of St Helen £1 0s 0d.
Staining church. From the tenements of William atte Gate and Richard Arnold 10s 0d.
Church of St James [Garlickhithe]. From the same tenements 2s 0d.

508. From the tenements of: Pykard to *Haliwell* 3s 4d; Richard Herewode to *Holy Trinity* 4s 0d; John Curteys to *the hospital of St Thomas* 3s 1d; the same to *Holy Trinity* 6s 9d.
Rents of: the crutched friars £4 13s 4d; the abbot of St Mary Graces £4 0s 0d.
Hospital of St Mary. From the tenements of: Edmund Olyver 4s 6d; John Govayre 18s 0d.
Rents of: the church of St Benet Paul's Wharf £2 13s 4d; a chantry of [St James] Garlickhithe (Garlykhithe) £1 9s 0d.

509. *Church of St Katherine.* From the tenements of Edmund Robur and Henry Robur 1s 0d. *Nuns of Stratford-at-Bow.* From the tenements of William Nicholas 1s 0d.
Rents of the abbot of St Mary Graces £2 14s 0d.
Holy Trinity. From the tenements of: Robert Norton 5s 0d; Philip Derneford £1 6s 0d; the same £1 5s 0d.
Rents of St Katherine £4 13s 4d.

510. [m. 9d] WALBROOK WARD.

Prior of Southwark. From the tenements of mr Richard Salyng 6s 0d.

Church of St John. From the tenements of: the same Richard £3 6s 8d; William Frammelyngham £1 0s 0d; Richard Arderne £1 0s 0d.

House of St Helen. From the same tenements £1 0s 0d.

St Michael Bassishaw (Bassyshawe). From the tenements which Walter Bewchamp holds 8s 0d.

Bermondsey. From the tenements of William Wyltschire 6s 8d.

Master of St Thomas of Acon. From the same tenements £2 8s 0d.

Church of St John. From the tenements of Adam Frannceys 13s 4d.

Prior of Holy Trinity. From the tenements of Thomas Blount 3s 6d.

Prior of the hospital of St Mary. From the tenements of John Walworth £1 0s 0d.

511. Rents of: the prior of the hospital of St Mary £23 12s 0d; the prior of Southwark £9 17s 4d.

From the tenements of Paul Salesbury to: *the prior of the hospital of St Mary* 5s 0d; *Southwark* 4s 6d; *Westminster* 5s 0d; *the prior of Merton* 5s 0d; *the prioress of Clerkenwell* 5s 0d; *the prior of Holy Trinity* 4s 6d.

Prior of Merton. From the tenements of John Sely 12s 0d.

Prior of Southwark. From the same tenements 3s 10d.

512. From a house of Robert Markley to: *the prior of Holy Trinity* 3s 0d; *the prioress of Stratford-at-Bow* 3s 0d; *'Stapwell' abbey* 6s 0d.

From the tenements of John Sely to: *the prioress of Clerkenwell* 13s 4d; *the abbot of St Albans* 3s 0d; *St Giles Holborn (Holeburn)* 3s 0d.

Rents of: the prior of Newark £4 0s 0d; the master of St Thomas of Acon £22 0s 0d; sir Roger Holme £13 6s 8d.

Prioress of Cheshunt. From the tenements which John Wosbeche holds 10s 0d.

513. *Bermondsey.* From the tenements of John Sibill 2s 0d.

Prioress of Clerkenwell. From the tenements of Thomas Mallyng £1 0s 0d.

Prior of Tortington (Tortolyngton). From the same tenements 4s 0d.

Prior of Holy Trinity. From the tenements: of Thomas Doushous 6s 0d; of Thomas Bastwold £1 0s 0d; which Sewale Hoddesdon holds £1 6s 8d.

Rents of the master of St Thomas of Acon £2 0s 0d.

Clerkenwell. From the tenements of Agnes Gemens £1 0s 0d.

Roger Holme. From the tenements of Thomas Bocock £5 0s 0d.

Clerkenwell. From the tenements of Robert Dane £4 0s 0d.

514. *Roger Holme.* From the tenements of John Lane £2 10s 0d.

Abbot of St Mary Graces. From the tenements of John Southcote £3 13s 4d.

Master of St James. From the same tenements 4d.

From the tenements of the master of St Thomas of Acon £4 4s 0d.

Church of St Swithin. Rents of the church £8 0s 8d; from the tenements of John Bokelsmyth 3s 4d.

Chapel of Watton. From the tenements of Richard Forster £3 6s 8d.

Church of St Swithin. From the tenements of: John Pellyng 10s 0d; John Prentys 3s 4d; the wife of John Walsshe 3s 4d.

515. *Holy Trinity.* From the tenements of Nicholas Hontot 13s 4d.
Rent of: St Helen £4 4s 8d; the prior of Tortington £14 10s 8d.
Church of St Swithin. From the tenements of William Burton 6s 8d.
Rents of the church of St Magnus £4 0s 0d.
Prior [sic] of Trowbridge (Troubrigge). From a house of Nicholas Merwe 1d.
[St] Michael Crooked Lane. From the tenement of William Perfit £2 13s 4d.
Prioress of Stratford-at-Bow. From the tenements of Richard Thondorbe
£1 0s 0d.
Master of the college of St Lawrence. From the tenements of Bartholomew
Neve £1 15s 4d.
[St Mary] Abchurch. From the tenements of John Halle 6s 8d.
Holy Trinity. From the same tenements 12s 0d.

516. *Church of St Paul.* Rents of St Paul £2 0s 0d; from the tenements of
John Donyngton 8s 0d.
Master of St Thomas of Acon. From the tenements of William Hoyston 5s 0d.
Church of St Dionis. From the tenements of Nicholas Taillour 13s 4d.
Prioress of Haliwell. From the tenements of John Salle 6s 8d.
Prioress of Cheshunt. From the tenements of John Gyle 6d.
Rents of the church of St Katherine £5 1s 0d.
Prior [sic] of Colchester. From the church of St Stephen Walbrook 10s 0d.
Rent of the church of [blank] which John Spark holds £3 0s 0d.

Total £169 15s 3d.

517. [m. 10] CRIPPLEGATE WARD WITHIN.
Rents of: St Martin le Grand £4 13s 4d; the church of St Lawrence which
John Otteley holds £20 0s 0d; the church of St James Garlickhithe
£11 6s 8d; the church of St Michael Wood Street (Hogenlane) £13 10s 4d;
sir Adam Brekespere dwelling in the church of St Olave £15 0s 0d; the
prior of Elsing Spital £20 10s 8d.
From the rent of the prior [sic] of St Helen £3 7s 0d.
Rents of: the dean and chapter of St Paul £20 7s 4d; the prioress of Haliwell
£2 0s 0d; the prior of the hospital of St Mary with rent of a canon of
St Paul £2 12s 0d; the church of St Lawrence which William Evote holds
£3 6s 8d.

518. Rents of: the abbot of Westminster £17 0s 0d; the prior of Elsing
Spital £23 6s 8d; the dean and chapter of St Paul £2 16s 0d; *note* the
hospital of St Bartholomew £10 0s 0d; the abbot of Lesnes £11 4s 0d;
mr Richard Wynwyk prebendary of Chrishall (Cresteshale) £6 13s 4d.
From rent of: the church of St Mary Magdalene £1 10s 0d; the same church
£4 12s 8d; the same church £6 12s 8d.
Rents of: a chantry of the church of St Paul £8 10s 0d; Tilty (Tiltey) abbey
£9 0s 0d.

519. Rents of: St Martin le Grand £3 6s 8d; the church of St Paul £4 13s 4d;
Tilty abbey £6 0s 0d; the church of St Michael £8 13s 4d; *note* the
minoresses (St Mary without Allgate) £3 6s 8d; *note* St Bartholomew

£4 0s 0d; sir Laurence chaplain £8 13s 4d; the prior of Holy Trinity £1 10s 0d; the minoresses £2 0s 0d; the prior of Holy Trinity £3 10s 0d; divers rectors whose names Gilbert Lirpe knows £10 13s 4d.

£273 15s 11d.

520. CRIPPLEGATE WARD WITHOUT.
St Paul. From the rent of Drew Barantyn 1s 0d.
Hospital of St Mary without Bishopsgate. From the rent of Edmund Fakenham 16s 4d.
[Friars] minor. From the tenement of William Poumfrat 9s 0d.
Dean of St Paul. From his garden £2 0s 0d.
Church of St Giles. From the tenement of William atte Gate 18s 0d.
Prior of Charterhouse. His rents £8 17s 8d.
From the tenements of Richard Kymbell to: *the hospital of St Mary* 10s 0d; *St Katherine* 4s 6d; *the church of St Giles* 4s 0d; *the church of St Paul* 1s 2d.

521. From the tenements of Nicholas Portour to: *the church of St Giles* 7s 0d; *the church of St Paul* 4d; *the prior of Newark* 3s 0d.
Church of St Paul. From the tenements of William Poumfreyt 1s 8d.
Clerkenwell. From the same tenements 2s 4d.
Dean of St Paul. From his tenement £3 4s 0d.
Finsbury (Fynesbery) of [St] Paul. From the rent of lord de Wilby £1 0s 0d.
Church of St Giles. From the same rent 3s 0d.
Prior of [St] Bartholomew. From the tenements of: Richard Redyng 5s 8d; John Vyaunt 8s 0d.

522. *Church of St Giles.* From the tenements of John Crowe £1 12s 0d.
Church of St Lawrence Pountney. From the same tenements 8s 0d.
Master of [St Thomas] of Acon. From the tenement of John Raulyn 8s 7d.
Church of St Mary Aldermanbury (Aldirmanbery). From the tenement of Gilbert Bonce 6s 8d.
Finsbury of [St] Paul. From the tenement of John Newport 4s 1d.
St Giles. From the tenement of Richard Kymbell 1s 0d.
Thrawbrigge vicar. From a tenement of sir John Throwbrygge vicar of St Giles £1 0s 0d.
Abbot of Ramsey (Rammeshay). From fifteen shops £3 7s 0d.
Dean of St Paul. From the tenement of Richard Forster £1 9s 0d.
Church of St Paul. From the tenements of Emmet Groome 1s 0d.
Church of St Giles. From the same tenements 1s 0d.

523. From a tenement of: John Hegme to *the prebendary of Mora* 1s 11d; *the prior of Newark* £1 4s 0d; Alice Austyne to *the church of St Giles* 16s 0d; Nicholas Taillour to *the prebend of Mora* 1s 10d; Robert Herymay to the same 2s 0d; the same Robert to *Haliwell* 4s 0d; the prior of Elsing Spital £1 4s 0d; the prior of Holy Trinity £2 0s 0d; Walter atte Hale to *the fraternity of St Giles* 7s 0d; Robert Heringay to *the prebend of Mora* 3s 10d.

524. From the tenements of: William Lightgrave to *the church* [blank] 2s 0d; Richard Seryne to *the prebend of Mora* 1s 10d; the prior of Newark £13 14s 4d; a chantry in the Guildhall (Guyhalde) £8 8s 8d; Gilbert Lirpe to *the master of St Thomas of Acon* 13s 4d; Lucy Enfeld to the *church of St Giles* 10s 0d; William Bome to *the fraternity of St Giles* 6s 8d; the same William to *the prebend of Mora* 2s 0d; John Wolfhay to the same 7s 6d; John Nasyng to *the hospital of St Mary* 10s 0d.

525. *Prebend of Mora.* From the rent of Thomas Hunte 2s 0d.
Prior of Holy Trinity. From the tenement of John Wolfhay £1 0s 0d.
From the tenements of: John Wykes to *the church of St Alphage* 10s 0d; the same John to *the church of St Paul* 3s 4d; John Bussh to *the prebend of Mora* 2s 0d; the abbot of Westminster £2 13s 4d; Henry Payne to *the prior of Holy Trinity* 12s 4d; John Wolfhay to *the church of St Giles* 9s 0d.
Chantry of St Peter Paul's Wharf. From the tenement which William Thomer holds £4 13s 4d.
London rectors. From the tenement of John Nasyng 6s 8d.

526. *Prebend of Mora.* From a garden £2 10s 0d.
From the tenements of: John Hogham to *the church of St Katherine* 2s 0d; the same to *the church of St Giles* 4d; John Lancastre to *the prebend of Mora* 4s 0d; Joan Mody to *the vicar of St Giles* 2s 0d; John Northehawe to *St Katherine* 2s 0d; John Philippe to *the church of St Giles* 1s 0d; Richard Kent to *St Katherine by the Tower* 1s 3d; William Haper to *the fraternity of St Giles* 1s 0d; William Thomer to *a minoress* 6s 8d; the same William to *the prebend of Mora* 8d; William Brounyng to the same 4d.

527. From the tenements of: John Phelipp to *the prior of* [St] *Bartholomew* 4s 0d; the same to *the prebend of Mora* 8d; Beatrice Phippe to *the church of St Giles* 6s 0d; the same Phippe to *the prebend of Mora* 4s 0d; John Trewbrigge vicar of St Giles £2 0s 0d; Robert Stooc to *the prebend of Mora* 10s 0d.
Abbot of Ramsey. A manor with six shops [blank]; from a tenement called Vynsentyshyve £2 13s 4d.
Vicar of St Giles. From a tenement of the vicar which formerly belonged to Matthew Assheby £8 0s 0d.
Fraternity of St Giles. From rent £9 6s 8d.
Trewbrigge vicar. From a tenement of John Trewbrigge vicar £11 0s 0d.

£382 10s 2d. [£106 14s 3d crossed through].

528. [m. 10d] CHEAP WARD.
Church of [St Mary Magdalene] *Milk Street* (*Melkestrete*). From the tenements of John Bosham 2s 0d.
Church of St Lawrence. From the tenement of William Parker 4s 0d.
Rents of: the abbess of Barking £7 0s 0d; the church of St James Garlickhithe £6 0s 0d; the church of St Lawrence £3 1s 4d; the prior of Elsing Spital £26 15s 0d; the same £19 0s 0d; the same £2 0s 0d; the abbess of the minoresses of Tower Hill £5 6s 8d; the prior of the hospital of St

Mary £8 5s 0d; the master of St Thomas of Acon £6 0s 0d; the prioress of Haliwell £3 0s 0d; the prioress of Clerkenwell £10 13s 4d; the prior of Newark £74 17s 8d; the minoresses of Tower Hill £16 11s 4d; the prior of Elsing Spital £26 16s 8d.

529. *Hospital of St Mary.* From the tenement of William Wroth £4 0s 0d. Rents of the prioress of Haliwell £5 0s 0d.
Hospital of St Mary. From the tenements of Robert Turk £3 6s 8d.
Rents of: the prior of Elsing Spital £12 0s 0d; the prior of St Bartholomew £22 16s 8d; the prior of Elsing Spital £12 6s 8d; the prior of St Bartholomew £4 0s 0d; the master of St Thomas of Acon £15 4s 0d; the rector of the church of [St Martin Pomery] Ironmonger Lane (Ysmongerelane) £3 0s 0d.

530. *Prioress of Kilburn.* From the rent of sir John Cifrewast £2 10s 0d.
From the same tenements to: *the prioress of Haliwell* £1 0s 0d; *Westminster* 10s 0d; *Martin [Pomery] Ironmonger Lane (Irmongerlane)* £5 16s 8d; *the prior of Merton* £3 16s 0d; *a certain monk* 6s 8d; *a certain chaplain* £1 13s 4d; *the church of St Katherine* £1 0s 0d; *the church of Holy Trinity* 5s 0d.
Cheshunt. From the tenements of lady Joan Pyell 5s 0d.

531. *Merton.* From the tenements of sir John Cifrewast £3 16s 0d.
St Katherine. From the tenements of the same John £1 0s 0d.
[St] Pancras. From the tenements of John Wade £1 5s 0d.
Bermondsey. From the tenements of the same 10s 0d.
John Yde rector. From his tenements £3 10s 0d.
Chantry of St Pancras. From the same tenements to a chaplain £1 6s 8d.
Church of St Paul. From the same tenements £3 6s 8d.
St Antonin. From the tenements of Hugh Middelton £3 0s 0d.
Dean of St Martin le Grand. Rents £22 17s 0d.
From the tenements of Adam Fraunceys £2 9s 0d.

532. Rents of: the prior of Elsing Spital £1 0s 0d; the prioress of Haliwell £3 0s 0d; the prior of Bermondsey £1 0s 0d; the church of St Mary le Bow (atte Bowe) £20 0s 0d.
Holy Trinity. From the tenements of Adam Fraunceys £5 7s 6d; from the corner of Ironmonger Lane £7 13s 4d.
Rents of: the master of St Thomas of Acon £46 8s 3d; the prior of Shouldham (Scholdham) £9 13s 4d; the prior of Chicksands (Checkeshand) £12 17s 8d; the hospital of St Mary 13s 4d.

533. *Holy Trinity.* From the tenement of sir Thomas Broun £6 13s 4d; rents of the prior £4 0s 0d.
From the tenements of William Evote to: *the church of St Paul* £3 0s 0d; *the hospital of St Mary* £1 6s 8d; *the master of St Thomas of Acon* 13s 4d.
Clerkenwell. From the tenements of: John Salle 13s 4d; William Horscroft £1 0s 0d.
Holy Trinity. From the tenements of John Derham £1 0s 0d.

Rents of: the prior of Shouldham £16 0s 0d; the prior of Chicksands £11 2s 8d; the prior of Elsing Spital £7 3s 4d; the church of St Paul £5 8s 0d.

534. From the tenements of Adam Fraunceys £8 9s 0d.
Prioress of Stratford-at-Bow. From the tenements of Thomas Medelane 3s 4d.
Minoress outside Aldgate. From the same tenements 13s 4d.
Church of St Giles. From the tenements of Henry Frank £2 0s 0d.
Haliwell. From the tenements of: lady Haveryng £6 6s 8d; Thomas Bocok £3 0s 0d.
[King's] Chapel Westminster. From the tenements of Maud Holbeche £20 0s 0d.[1]
From the tenements of Adam Fraunceys to: *Haliwell* £3 0s 0d; *Westminster* 3s 4d; *Cheshunt* 10s 0d.

1. The taxation column has 3s 4d.

535. *Hospital of St Giles.* From the tenements of John Wallcote £1 0s 0d.
Holy Trinity. From the same tenements £1 0s 0d.
St Giles. From the rent of Alice Holbeche £1 0s 0d.
Church of St Paul. Rents £6 13s 4d.
Hospital of St Mary. From the tenements of William Horston £1 6s 8d.
Chantry of St Benet. From the same tenements to a priest of St Benet £4 0s 0d.
Hospital of St Mary. From the tenements of Maud Holbeche 13s 4d.
Balliol Hall (Bailhall) Oxford. From the tenement of Simon Wurstede £4 0s 0d.

£587 4s 1d.

536. [m. 11] DOWGATE WARD (Dougate).
PARISH OF ST LAWRENCE POUNTNEY.
From the tenement of William atte Lee which Thomas Brustowe holds to the prior of the hospital of St Mary without Bishopsgate 8s 0d.
Rents of the prior of Holy Trinity worth p.a. £6 10s 8d.
Rent which Richard Gylberd holds of a college [sic] in the church of St Paul worth p.a. £10 13s 4d.
Without. From the tenements: of John Tettusbury to the prior of Elsing Spital 12s 0d; *memorandum* which William Parker holds from the church of St Peter Westcheap worth p.a. [blank]; of William Wytton' to the church of St Michael Crooked Lane £3 6s 8d; of the same to the bishop of Winchester 1s 8d; Robert Chircheman to the hospital of St John Clerkenwell (without Smythfeld) £2 0s 0d.

537. PARISH OF ALL HALLOWS THE LESS.
From the tenements of: Henry Vannere to the church of St Dunstan £9 6s 8d; the same to Southwark priory 6s 0d; Roger Marchal to the bishop of Winchester £2 13s 4d; *Note* John Colpeper to the hospital of St Bartholomew £3 6s 8d; the same to the church of St Lawrence Pountney 10s 0d; Simon Benfeld to the bishop of Winchester £1 6s 8d.

75

Note. Rents of: the church of St Lawrence Pountney £8 0s 0d; the hospital of St Bartholomew £13 6s 0d.

From the tenement of Reginald Cobbeham to the church[1] [sic] of St John Haliwell £2 13s 4d.

Rents of the master of St Thomas of Acon £4 0s 0d.

1. 'Hospital' crossed through.

538. PARISH OF ALL HALLOWS THE GREAT.

From the tenement of Thomas Wyght to the church of All Hallows the Great £3 6s 8d.

Rents of: brother Walter Durant belonging to Dartford £8 13s 4d; the church of All Hallows the Less £1 6s 8d; John Cosyn chaplain £13 6s 8d; Southwark priory £8 0s 0d; the abbot of St Mary Graces £2 0s 0d; the prior of the hospital of St Mary without Bishopsgate £2 13s 4d.

From the tenement of Gilbert Purveys to: the church of St Antonin £2 0s 0d; the church of St Paul £1 6s 8d; the hospital of St Bartholomew 10s 0d; the abbot of Westminster 5s 0d.

From the tenement of John Chartesey to the church of All Hallows the Great 13s 4d.

Rents of the crutched friars of London £3 0s 0d.

539. PARISH OF ST MICHAEL PATERNOSTER.

From the tenements of: Andrew Newport to the same church of St Michael £1 0s 0d; *memorandum* Agnes atte Hale £1 10s 0d; James de Billyngford to the church of St John Walbrook 16s 0d; Roger Cheyne to the nuns of Kilburn £1 0s 0d.

Rents of the master of the hospital of St Katherine £3 0s 0d.

540. PARISH OF ST JOHN WALBROOK.

Rents of the nuns [sic] of Tower Hill £10 5s 8d.

From the tenement of Thomas Swynbourne chivaler to the prior of Holy Trinity £1 0s 0d.

£133 16s 0d.

541. PORTSOKEN WARD (Portsokene).

From the tenements of: the prior of Holy Trinity which William Haveray holds 13s 4d; the same prior 13s 4d; William Dawe to the same prior 9s 3d; William Belhomme to the same prior 6s 0d; the same prior which Thomas Saham holds 2s 4d; Richard Skynner to the same prior 2s 6d; Robert Rysby to the same prior 2s 6d; Thomas Ham' for the master of the house (magistro hous), to the same prior 1s 6d; the prior of the hospital of St Mary without Bishopsgate 10s 0d; the prior of Holy Trinity £7 0s 0d; Robert Bureford to the same prior 8s 4d; John Syverwas for Ad' Stable to the same prior 2s 6d; the same to the church of St John Walbrook 9s 0d.

542. From the tenements of: the prior of Holy Trinity £1 0s 0d; Nicholas Longe to the same prior 3s 6d; John Rawleyn to the same prior 7d; the church of St Michael Bassishaw £5 0s 0d; the same to the prior of Holy Trinity 5s 0d; *abbot Grac'* the abbot of St Mary Graces £4 0s 0d; the same to the prior of Holy Trinity 2s 0d; Thomas Clerk to the same prior 14s 10d; Henry atte Hoke to the same prior 1s 0d; John Sexoy to the same prior 4s 0d.

Memorandum from the tenement of: John Hawkeyn and the church of St Botolph 16s 0d; the same to the prior of Holy Trinity 1s 4d; item to the church of St Botolph 4s 0d.

543. From the tenements of: mr William de Turre to the bishop of London 2s 0d; Thomas Morekoc(?) to the minoresses 16s 0d; the abbot of St Mary Graces £3 0s 0d; Thomas Clerk to the prior of Holy Trinity 1s 9d; Roger Ryot to the same prior 1s 9d; the same prior 13s 4d; John Godrom to the same prior 3s 2d; the same prior concerning the chantry of John Romeneye £7 6s 8d; the same to a chaplain celebrating for the same chantry £4 0s 0d; the same 7s 2½d; the same to the church of St Botolph £1 0s 0d; the same to the church of All Hallows Honey Lane 8s 10d; the same to the nuns of St Helen 4s 0d.

544. From the tenements of: the abbess of St Clare [sic] £7 6s 8d; the same to the prior of Holy Trinity 17s 9½d; the prior of Holy Trinity 13s 4d; Thomas Felawe to the hospital of St Katherine 2s 0d;[1] Nicholas Longe to the prior of Holy Trinity 1s 0d; Thomas Felaw to the same prior 1s 0d; the same to the hospital of St Katherine 2s 0d;[1] John Sexoy to the prior of Holy Trinity 1s 0d; John Bally to the same prior 6d; the same to the hospital of St Mary without Bishopsgate 4s 0d; Stephen Flecher to the prior of Holy Trinity 6s 0d; Agnes Fannere to the same prior 7s(?) 5d.

1. There is an axe drawn in the margin beside each of these items.

545. From the tenements of: the hospital of St Katherine £1 4s 0d; the nuns of St Helen £1 4s 0d; the same to the prior of Holy Trinity 5s 0d; the abbot of Coggeshall (Coggeshale) £6 10s 0d; the same to the prior of Holy Trinity 5s 6d; John Somersham to the same prior 1s 6d; *note* the abbot of St Mary Graces £18 0s 0d; the same to the prior of Holy Trinity 2s 6d; *note* the master of the hospital of St Katherine £10 0s 0d; [blank] Vascombe to the abbot of St Mary Graces 1s 4d; the same abbot £7 13s 4d; the master of the hospital of St Katherine £10 0s 0d.

546. [m. 11d] Note concerning the rent of the abbot of St Mary Graces on this roll on the other side [i.e. **542**].

ACTA OF WILLIAM COURTENAY,
BISHOP OF LONDON, 1375–81

547. Memorandum that on 1 December 1375 William bishop of London appeared in person before William bishop of Winchester in his manor of Esher, Winchester diocese, and showed the bishop of Winchester his bull of translation, dated 13 September 1375, addressed to the bishops of Winchester and Rochester ordering them to receive the oath of obedience of the new bishop of London in order to spare him the journey to the *curia*. Thereupon the new bishop took the oath of obedience to the holy see in the form prescribed in the bull. [Reg. Wykeham i f.68v]

548. Certificate of execution of the commission of John bishop of Lincoln, dated 3 December 1375, for the exchange between John Burleye vicar of Stepney (Stebenhithe), London diocese, and Nicholas Dene rector of Harpole (Horpole), Lincoln diocese. Sealed with 'the seal which we used in the diocese of Hereford', Barnes (Mawode Bernes iuxta London) 5 December 1375. [L.A.O. Reg. 10 f.202]

549. Certificate of Adam Mottrum vicar-general of William bishop of London in his absence, of execution of the commission of John bishop of Lincoln, dated 6 February 1376, for the exchange between John de Burton rector of Dunton Waylett (Dunton), London diocese, and Simon de Legh rector of Grafham (Grofham), Lincoln diocese. London 10 February 1376, 'under the seal of the officiality which is to hand.' [*Ibid.* f. 311v]

550. Certificate of mr Adam Mottrum, vicar-general in spirituals in the absence of William bishop of London, of execution of the commission of Ralph bishop of Salisbury, dated 10 February 1376, for the exchange between Adam de Hertyngdon canon of Salisbury and prebendary of Netheravon (Netheravene), and John de Bisshoppeston rector, chaplain, or warden of the chapel of Sheering (Shyryng), London diocese. Given under the seal of the officiality of London 13 February 1376. [Salisbury diocesan record office, Reg. Erghum ff. 16v–17]

551. Certificate of Adam Mottrum vicar-general in the absence of William bishop of London, of execution of the commission of John bishop of Lincoln, dated 20 February 1376, for the exchange between William Dale vicar of Rushden (Rushenden), Lincoln diocese, and Thomas le Skynnere chaplain of the perpetual chantry of Puckeridge, London diocese. London 25 February 1376. [L.A.O. Reg. 10 ff. 311–311v]

552. Certificate of Adam Mottrum vicar-general in spirituals during the absence of William bishop of London, of execution of the commission of John bishop of Lincoln, dated 7 March 1376, for the exchange between Adam Hargrave rector of a moiety of Danbury, London diocese, and Hugh Knyght rector of Oving (Ovyng), Lincoln diocese. London 19 March 1376. [*Ibid.* f. 438v]

553. Mandate to William bishop of Winchester to execute the summons of Simon archbishop of Canterbury, dated 3 May 1376, to a meeting of convocation of the clergy of the southern province in St Paul's cathedral on 9 June 1376. London 5 May 1376. [Reg. Wykeham ii ff. 138v–139v]

554. Mandate to Thomas bishop of Ely to collect $1\frac{1}{2}$d in the mark on all benefices as procurations for Pileus archbishop of Ravenna, William archbishop of Rouen and mr Giles Sanctii Munionis provost of Valencia papal nuncios to England and Flanders, and their notaries, the money to be paid before 7 July 1376 to Robert rector of St Gregory, London, along with any arrears of procurations imposed during the time of Simon archbishop of Canterbury. London 7 May 1376. [Reg. Arundel (Ely) f. 16]

555. Signification that mr Nicholas Chaddesden, excommunicated for contumacy, has remained obdurate for forty days and more. London 29 May 1376. [C85/122 no. 1]

556. Commission to Henry bishop of Worcester to effect the exchange between Roger de Beauchamp rector of Minchinhampton, Worcester diocese, and William Potyn rector of High Ongar, London diocese. London 8 June 1376. [*Reg. Wakefeld* no. 31]

557. Commission to Henry bishop of Worcester to effect the exchange between William Goldsmyth vicar of Ampney Crucis, Worcester diocese, and Reginald Sperner custodian of St Mary's chantry in the church of St Michael le Querne, London. London 21 June 1376. [*Ibid.* no. 35]

558. a. Exchequer writ of *venire faciatis*, dated 26 May 1376, returnable on 25 June against John Capel rector of Dunmow an executor of the will of Lionel duke of Clarence and an occupier of the manor of la Doos in the town of Standon, Herts., to answer the crown and Bartholomew Pyket kt another of the duke's executors and occupiers of the manor for the profits of the manor from 15 August 1369 to 15 August 1370.
b. [face] Return to the exchequer barons of the annexed writ certifying that the bishop has caused John Capel rector of Dunmow to be warned to appear before them on the day named in the writ and to do what it demands. London 25 June 1376. [dorse] Note that John Capel appeared in the exchequer on the day named. [E202/60 pt 1 file 1 top pile bundle 2 no. 2]

559. Certificate of execution of the commission of John bishop of Lincoln, dated 20 June 1376, for the exchange between William Cudy rector of St Mary Somerset, London, and Simon Tuk' rector of Morborne, Lincoln diocese. London 26 June 1376. [L.A.O. Reg. 10 f. 312v]

560. Signification that John Fannewright of Writtle (Wrytele), London diocese, excommunicated for contumacy, has remained obdurate for forty days and more. London 10 July 1376. [C85/122 no. 2]

561. Certificate of execution of the commission of John bishop of Lincoln, dated 12 July 1376, for the exchange between John Coupere rector of Chickney (Chikeneye), London diocese, and William de Wetherfeld vicar of Great Gransden (Grantesden Magna), Lincoln diocese, and that William has been put into possession of Great Gransden in the person of his proctor mr John de Potton bachelor of canon law, rector of Hatley St George (Hattele St George), Ely diocese. Stepney 20 July 1376. [L.A.O. Reg. 10 f. 313]

562. Certificate of execution of the commission of John bishop of Lincoln, dated 22 October 1376, for the exchange between mr Roger Sutton rector of Glatton, Lincoln diocese, and William Rysyng rector of Black Notley (Nigra Nottele), London diocese. London palace 23 October 1376. [*Ibid.* f. 313v]

563. Signification that John Fitzrauf of London diocese, excommunicated for contumacy, has remained obdurate for forty days and more. London 27 October 1376. [C85/122 no. 3]

564. William bishop of London acting on a commission of Simon archbishop of Canterbury, dated 24 October 1376, effected the exchange between Nicholas Fornham perpetual vicar of Herne, Canterbury diocese, and mr Roger Sutton rector of Black Notley (Nigra Notlee), London diocese. London palace 27 October 1376. [Reg. Sudbury (Cant.) f. 119v]

565. Certificate of execution of the commission of William bishop of Winchester, dated 31 October 1376, for the exchange between Hugh de Woketon rector of St Margaret Pattens, London diocese, and John Houghton of Swineshead (Swyneshened) rector of Long Ditton (Longe-ditton) Winchester diocese. London palace 2 November 1376. [Reg. Wykeham i f. 79]

566. Mandate to William bishop of Winchester to execute the order of Simon archbishop of Canterbury dated 27 October 1376, for prayers for peace to be said throughout the diocese, with a grant of forty days' indulgence to those present. London 2 November 1376. [Reg. Wykeham ii f. 147v]

567. Commission to Thomas bishop of Exeter to effect the exchange between John Stephyn chaplain of the chantry in the free chapel of St Michael in the cemetery of St Austell (St Austol), Exeter diocese, and Philip Roger vicar of Great Bentley (Bentley Magna), London diocese. London palace 5 November 1376. [Reg. Brantingham ii f. 45]

568. Mandate to William bishop of Winchester to execute the summons of

Simon archbishop of Canterbury, dated 17 December 1376, to a meeting of convocation of the clergy of the southern province in St Paul's cathedral on 3 February 1377. Wickham manor 23 December 1376. [Reg. Wykeham ii ff. 148v–149]

569. Letter to a cardinal[1] informing him that through the action of certain enemies the bishop of Winchester has, by process of a secular court, been deprived of his possessions and manors; and begging the cardinal to take a stand against these detractors if they should malign the bishop at the *curia*. [Undated] [*John Lydford's Book* no. 178]

    1. Probably Simon Langham, to whom Lydford's previous letter was addressed.

570. Another letter on the same subject. London 7 January 1377. [*Ibid.* no. 179]

571. Signification that Ralph Taillor dwelling in the parish of St Thomas the Apostle and William Scrivener staying in the parish of St Sepulchre in our jurisdiction, London, excommunicated for their contumacies in not coming before the president of our consistory of London, have remained obdurate for forty days and more. London 20 January 1377. [C85/122 no. 4]

572. Signification that Ralph Daventry, clerk, of London diocese, excommunicated for contumacy in not coming before the president of our consistory, has remained obdurate for forty days and more. London palace 4 February 1377. [*Ibid.* no. 5]

573. Signification that Ralph Daventry, clerk, of London diocese, excommunicated for contumacy in not coming before the president of our consistory, has remained obdurate for forty days and more. London palace 8 February 1377. [*Ibid.* no. 6]

574. Commission to John bishop of Lincoln to effect the exchange between William Trufford rector of Wymington (Wymyngton), Lincoln diocese, and Robert Lamborne (or Lambourne) rector of Wimbish (Wymbissh), London diocese. London palace 9 February 1377. [L.A.O. Reg. 10 ff. 394–394v]

575. Commission to Ralph bishop of Salisbury to effect the exchange between Robert Marr rector of West Kington (Westkyngton), Salisbury diocese, and John Wyke rector of South Hanningfield (Southunyngfeld), London diocese. London 22 February 1377. [Salisbury diocesan record office, Reg. Erghum f. 24v]

576. Mandate to Thomas bishop of Ely to execute the order of Simon archbishop of Canterbury, dated 4 March 1377, for the collection of arrears of procurations to William archbishop of Rouen, Pileus archbishop of Ravenna and mr Giles Munionis provost of Valencia, the money to be paid to Henry Wylowes rector of St [Nicholas] Olave, London and the bishop to certify to the collector by letters patent the actions he had taken in this matter. London palace 6 March 1377. [Reg. Arundel (Ely) ff. 82–82v]

577. Mr John Codeford doctor of laws vicar-general in spirituals of William bishop of London who is outside his diocese, acting on a commission of Simon archbishop of Canterbury, dated 5 May 1377, effected the exchange between Edmund Harendenne vicar of Bethersden (Beatrichisdenne), Canterbury diocese, and Richard Kynet vicar of Walthamstow (Welcoum-stowe), London diocese. 9 May 1377. [Reg. Sudbury (Cant.) f. 121v]

578. Mandate to William bishop of Winchester to execute the order of Simon archbishop of Canterbury, dated 23 May 1377, to collect 1d in the £ on all benefices as procuration for mr Giles provost of Valencia at the rate of six florins a day, and five florins a day for his notary, the money to be paid to the collector Henry Wylows rector of St [Nicholas] Olave London by 29 September. London 14 June 1377. [Reg. Wykeham ii ff. 153v–55]

579. Signification that Richard Bronde staying in the parish of St Swithin, London, in our jurisdiction, excommunicated for contumacy, has remained obdurate for forty days and more. London 30 June 1377. [C85/122 no. 7]

580. Commission to John bishop of Lincoln to effect the exchange between Stephen Percy rector of Manby, Lincoln diocese, and Walter de Gretham rector of Dengie (Dengay), London diocese. London 25 July 1377. [L.A.O. Reg. 10 f. 86v]

581. Commission to John bishop of Lincoln to effect the exchange between William Risyng rector of Glatton, Lincoln diocese, and Richard Depedale rector of Ingatestone (Gynge ad Petram, Gynge atte Stone), London diocese. London 7 August 1377. [*Ibid.* f. 316]

582. Mandate to William bishop of Winchester to execute the summons of Simon archbishop of Canterbury, dated 4 October 1377, to a meeting of convocation of the clergy of the southern province in St Paul's cathedral on 9 November 1377. London 10 October 1377. [Reg. Wykeham ii ff. 157v–158]

583. Signification that John Bilney of London diocese, excommunicated for contumacy, has remained obdurate for forty days and more. Fulham 10 October 1377. [C85/122 no. 8]

584. Notification that William bishop of London has appointed Nicholas Hilderston and Thomas Payne as his attorneys to receive on his behalf two acres of land in the parish of Datchworth (Thachworth) in the field called 'Pynpeford', in Hertfordshire, along with the advowson of North Mimms (Northmymmes) church in the same county, which two acres and advowson he and Richard II lately purchased from Nicholas de Thornton and Thomas Bedewyn clerks, to hold to themselves and their heirs according to the force, form and effect of a certain charter made for them by the said Nicholas de Thornton and Thomas Bedewyn. London 3 November 1377. [L.R. 2/61 ff. 153–153v]

585. Certificate of execution of the mandate of Simon archbishop of

Canterbury [dated 4 October 1377] to summon the clergy of the southern province to a meeting of convocation, with the names of those cited in the diocese of London contained on an annexed schedule. Fulham 9 November 1377. [Reg. Sudbury (Cant.) f. 44 without schedule]

586. Commission to Thomas bishop of Durham to effect the exchange between John Bowryng chaplain, canon and prebendary of Medomsley (Medmeslee) in Lanchester college, Durham diocese, and John Brokeman warden of the free chapel of St Margaret Chelmsford, London diocese. Fulham manor 9 December 1377. [Durham, Prior's Kitchen, Reg. Hatfield f. 127v]

587. Certificate of execution of the commission of William bishop of Winchester, dated 1 December 1377, for the exchange between Peter Chekyn chaplain of the perpetual chantry in All Hallows Barking (Berkyngchurch), London, and Richard Gretton perpetual vicar of Carshalton (Kersalton), and of receipt of an oath from Peter Chekyn that he would reside according to the constitutions of Otho and Ottobon. Fulham manor 11 December 1377. [Reg. Wykeham i ff. 89v–90]

588. Notification that William bishop of London and Richard Warmyngton clerk have appointed Thomas Payne and Thomas Veal as their attorneys to receive on their behalf seisin of two acres of land with appurtenances in Great Staughton (Stokton Magna), Huntingdonshire, together with the advowson of Staughton which Thomas de Welle of Norfolk by a charter gave to Richard II and themselves. London 16 December 1377. [W.A.M. no. 5092]

589. Quitclaim by William Curteney bishop of London to Richard II his heirs and assigns of all his rights in two acres of land in the parish of Datchworth in the field called 'Parva Pynkeford', in Hertfordshire, along with the advowson of North Mimms church with all rights and appurtenances, which he and the king purchased from Nicholas de Thornton and Thomas Bedewynd clerks. [No place] 2 January 1378. [L.R. 2/61 f. 153v]

590. Certificate of execution of the commission of John bishop of Lincoln, dated 2 December 1377, for the exchange between Peter Wynestede vicar of Ware, London diocese, and Philip Herteford rector of Aspenden (Aspeden), Lincoln diocese. Fulham manor 9 January 1378. [L.A.O. Reg. 10 f. 317v]

591. Certificate of execution of the commission of William bishop of Winchester, dated 27 January 1378, for the exchange between William Boyle perpetual vicar of Bedfont (Bedfunt), London diocese, and Alan de Shutyntone perpetual vicar of Ashtead (Ashtede), Winchester diocese. Fulham manor 31 January 1378. [Reg. Wykeham i ff. 92–92v]

592. Signification that John Hilhale layman of our diocese, excommunicated for contumacy, has remained obdurate for forty days and more. Fulham manor 5 February 1378. [C85/122 no. 9]

593. Licence to Thomas bishop of Exeter to celebrate both major and minor orders in the diocese of London when and where he chooses, both in his chapels and elsewhere, and to dedicate high altars and last sacraments (altar' maiora ac viatica), and, in his absence, for divine service to be celebrated for his household by suitable chaplains. Fulham manor 18 February 1378. [Reg. Brantingham ii f. 47v second sequence]

594. Commission to William bishop of Winchester to effect the exchange between John de Waltham rector of Bradwell [near the Sea], London diocese, and Peter de Burton clerk prebendary of Leckford church in the monastery of St Mary Winchester. Fulham manor 2 July 1378. [Reg. Wykeham ii f. 95]

595. Mandate to Thomas bishop of Ely to publish the letter of Simon archbishop of Canterbury, dated 23 August 1378, denouncing those persons unknown who violated the sanctuary of Westminster on 11 August last. London 28 August 1378. [Reg. Arundel (Ely) f. 86]

596. Certificate of execution of the commission of William bishop of Winchester, dated 23 September 1378, for the exchange between John Colyn rector of All Hallows London Wall, London diocese, and William Bakere perpetual vicar of Battersea (Batricheseye). London 26 September 1378. [Reg. Wykeham i ff. 96v–97]

597. William bishop of London acting on a commission of Simon archbishop of Canterbury, dated 29 November 1378, effected the exchange between Richard Calle priest of Salisbury diocese rector of Mersham (Merseham), Canterbury diocese, and John de Cressyngham rector of [Bishop's] Wickham, London diocese. London 29 November 1378. [Reg. Sudbury (Cant.) f. 127v]

598. William bishop of London effected the exchange between John Stanesfeld priest, represented by his proctor John Brocman, rector of Bocking (Bockyng), in the immediate jurisdiction of the archbishop of Canterbury, and Thomas Crocer priest [rector] of Sible Hedingham (Sibile Hedyngham), London diocese. London 6 December 1378. [*Ibid*. f. 127v]

599. Commission to William bishop of Winchester to effect the exchange between Thomas de Henyngham, priest, rector of Belchamp Otton (Belchamp Otto), London diocese, and John Spenser of Misterton, clerk, rector of Widley (Wydelegh), Winchester diocese. Wickham manor 16 December 1378. [Reg. Wykeham i ff. 97v–98]

600. Certificate of execution of the commission of William bishop of Winchester, dated 18 January 1379, for the exchange between John Felet perpetual chaplain of a certain chantry in St Dunstan in the West, London diocese, and John de Staunton rector of Woodmansterne (Wodemerston), Winchester diocese. Wickham manor 20 January 1379. [*Ibid*. ff. 98v–99]

601. Commission to John bishop of Lincoln to effect the exchange between Thomas Kymbelle rector of All Saints Broughton, Lincoln diocese, and John Amy rector of St Olave Old Jewry with the annexed chapel of St Stephen Coleman Street, London diocese. Wickham 28 January 1379. [L.A.O. Reg. 10 f. 319]

602. William bishop of London acting on a commission of Simon archbishop of Canterbury, dated 21 February 1379, effected the exchange between John Draycote vicar of Orpington (Orpynton), in the immediate jurisdiction of the archbishop of Canterbury, and William Amory priest [rector] of Chignall St James (Chickenhale Jamys), London diocese. Fulham manor 24 February 1379. [Reg. Sudbury (Cant.) f. 128]

603. Commission to John bishop of Lincoln to effect the exchange between John Petyt rector of Tewin (Tuwyng), Lincoln diocese, and John Herthill rector of Little Birch (Brich Parva), London diocese. London palace 8 March 1379 [L.A.O. Reg. 10 ff. 319v–320]

604. Commission to William bishop of Winchester to effect the exchange between William Jolyf rector of Little Laver (Laufare Parva), London diocese, and John Lord rector of North Waltham, Winchester diocese. Fulham manor 12 March 1379. [Reg. Wykeham i f. 99v]

605. Commission to Thomas bishop of Exeter to effect the exchange between Henry Pak perpetual chaplain of the chapel of St Michael in the cemetery of St Austell in Cornwall, Exeter diocese, and Richard Whitefote rector of the parish church of St Leonard, Beaumont (Bellemount), London diocese. Fulham manor 29 March 1379. [Reg. Brantingham ii ff. 56v–57]

606. Mandate to William bishop of Winchester to execute the summons of Simon archbishop of Canterbury, dated 21 March 1379, to a meeting of convocation of the clergy of the southern province in St Paul's cathedral on 9 May 1379. Fulham manor 31 March 1379. [Reg. Wykeham ii ff. 174v–175]

607. Mandate to Thomas bishop of Exeter to execute the order of Simon archbishop of Canterbury, dated 30 May 1379, to bring to the notice of all the faithful the bull of Urban VI 'Nuper cum Vinea' denouncing the antipope Robert of Geneva and his adherents, issued 6 November 1378. Fulham manor 4 May 1379. Present: mr Adam Mottrum and Thomas de Neylonde clerks of Lichfield and Norwich dioceses. Attested by John Prophete clerk of St Davids diocese, public and apostolic notary. [Reg. Brantingham ii ff. 27v–29 second sequence]

608. Signification that Alice Pykot wife of John Pykot of Halstead (Halsted), staying in Colchester, excommunicated for contumacy in not appearing before our commissary, has remained obdurate for forty days and more. Fulham manor 16 May 1379. [C85/122 no. 11]

609. Certificate of execution of the commission of John bishop of Lincoln, dated 19 May 1379, for the exchange between Nicholas Deene (or Dene) vicar of Stepney, London diocese, and Gilbert Drayton rector of Warkton (Werketon), Lincoln diocese. London palace 20 May 1379. [L.A.O. Reg. 10 f. 212v]

610. Certificate of execution of the commission of Henry bishop of Norwich, dated 16 May 1379, for the exchange between John Hened of Haslingfield (Haselyngfeld) rector of Sandon, London diocese, and William Batayle rector of Worlington (Wrydelyngton), Norwich diocese. London palace 23 May 1379. [Bodl. Libr. MS Film 651 ff. 63v–64]

611. Signification that John Balle chaplain, excommunicated for contumacy, has remained obdurate for forty days and more. Fulham manor 22 June 1379. [C85/122 no. 10]

612. Commission to John bishop of Lincoln to effect the exchange between Thomas de Wetewang rector of Tyringham (Tiryngham), Lincoln diocese, and John Baroun rector of Doddinghurst (Doddynghurst), London diocese. London 1 July 1379. [L.A.O. Reg. 10 f. 447v]

613. Signification that Hugh Grymhull of Great Bentley (Benteley Magna) in our diocese, excommunicated for contumacy in not appearing before us, has remained obdurate for forty days and more. Wickham manor 6 July 1379. [C85/122 no. 12]

614. Certificate of execution of the commission of John bishop of Lincoln, dated 6 July 1379, for the exchange between Robert Catour rector of Fryerning (Yeng Hospitalis), London diocese, and John Duffeld keeper of the free chapel of St John Baptist of Colne (Colneye), Lincoln diocese. Wickham manor 10 July 1379. [L.A.O. Reg. 10 ff. 322v–323]

615. Return to a writ of 'enquiretis de bastardia' in accordance with which William Robetot named in the writ and others were called and diligent enquiry made for the truth; it was found that John Hauchach named in the writ is not a bastard but was and is the legitimate son of Thomas Hauchach and Margaret his wife whose marriage was solemnized in church. Wickham manor 27 July 1379. [E135/7/8]

616. Commission to John bishop of Hereford to effect the exchange between John Worteley rector of Winforton (Wynfreton), Hereford diocese, and William Mody rector of Stock (Herewardestoke), London diocese. London palace 4 September 1379. [Hereford diocesan registry, Reg. Gilbert f. 5v]

617. Rescript, addressed to Henry bishop of Worcester, of the reissue of the constitution 'Effrenata' by Simon archbishop of Canterbury, dated 6 September 1379, by which the maximum wage for priests without cure of souls was fixed at 7 marks per annum, and for priests with cure of souls at 8 marks per annum. Fulham manor 18 September 1379. [*Reg. Wakefield* no. 841. The constitution is printed in full in several places, for example, D. Wilkins, *Concilia*, iii (1737), 135, wrongly dated.]

618. Commission to Robert bishop of Coventry and Lichfield to effect the exchange between Hugh de Piriton rector of Bonsall (Bondeshale), Coventry and Lichfield diocese, and Thomas Nichol rector of Woodham Walter (Wodeham Water), London diocese. Wickham manor 10 November 1379. [*The First Register of Robert de Stretton*, ed. R. A. Wilson (William Salt Archaeological Society, N.S., x, pt. 2, 1907), 96]

619. Mandate to Henry bishop of Worcester to execute the summons of Simon archbishop of Canterbury, dated 3 December 1379, to a meeting of convocation of the clergy of the southern province in St Paul's cathedral on 4 February 1380. Wickham 12 December 1379. [*Reg. Wakefeld* no. 842]

620. Certificate of execution of the commission of John bishop of Lincoln, dated 19 December 1379, for the exchange between Richard Daventre vicar of South Mimms (Southmymmes), London diocese, and Thomas Wylford vicar of Hemel Hempstead (Hemalhemstead), Lincoln diocese. Wickham manor 23 December 1379. [L.A.O. Reg. 10 ff. 323v–324]

621. Certificate of execution of the mandate of Simon archbishop of Canterbury [dated 3 December 1379], received 7 December 1379, to summon the clergy of the southern province to a meeting of convocation, with the names of those cited in the diocese of London contained on an annexed schedule. Fulham manor 31 December 1379. [Reg. Sudbury (Cant.) f. 60 without schedule]

622. Licence to Thomas bishop of Exeter to proceed anywhere in the city or diocese of London in the business of the election to Plympton priory, of the order of St Augustine, vacant by the death of bro Ralph Persoun the last prior; to enquire into, and to confirm or invalidate (infirmare) the election of bro John Shaldon priest and professed canon of the house. Fulham manor 3 February 1380. [Reg. Brantingham ii f. 59v]

623. Commission to John bishop of Lincoln to effect the exchange between William Jacob vicar of Stantonbury (Stonton Barry), Lincoln diocese, and William Beverache vicar of Willingale Spain (Wylynghale Andrew), London diocese. Fulham 12 February 1380. [L.A.O. Reg. 10 f. 448]

624. Licence to John bishop of Hereford to celebrate both major and minor orders on Ember Saturday in Chelsea (Chelchiche) parish church or in his London house (manso vestro). Fulham manor 17 February 1380. [Hereford diocesan registry, Reg. Gilbert f. 4]

625. Certificate of execution of the commission of John bishop of Lincoln, dated 27 February 1380, for the exchange between Thomas Lygh perpetual vicar of Sawbridgeworth (Sabrichworth), London diocese, and John de Brunne rector of Higham Gobion (Hygham Gobyon), Lincoln diocese. Fulham manor 5 March 1380. [L.A.O. Reg. 10 f. 398v]

626. Ratification and confirmation of a charter of Simon bishop of London,[1] dated 10 December 1374, establishing a chapel on the island of Foulness with provision for daily celebrations for the souls of William Bohun once earl of Northampton, Humphrey his son late earl of Hereford, and all their progenitors and successors, and Simon de Sudberia bishop of London; the chaplain to have the power to hear confessions and impose penances, to baptise infants, bury the dead, perform marriages and the purification of women; and to be paid from the oblations and tithes by the inhabitants of the island. Fulham manor 16 March 1380. Copied out of ye old Register-Booke in ye possession of Michael Harland vicar of Hockley 12 July 1708 per me Carolum Tyrells. [Essex Record Office D/DU 610 pp. 274-6]

1. Not entered in his register.

627. Commission to John bishop of Lincoln to effect the exchange between Richard Porter rector of Quinton (Quynton), Lincoln diocese, and William Furnays rector of Little Ilford (Parva Ilford), London diocese. London 20 March 1380. [L.A.O. Reg. 10 ff. 217–217v]

628. Return, to the treasurer and barons of the exchequer, of the writ of 6 March 1380, ordering collection of a subsidy of 16d in the mark on all assessed benefices, 16d in the mark on two-thirds of the value of non-assessed benefices, and 2s 0d each from all other priests, advocates, proctors, registrars and notaries public, whose terms are 3 May and 24 June, the names of collectors to be certified by 12 March. Certification that he has appointed as collector from the dean and chapter and other ecclesiastical persons of the cathedral Richard Pyryton archdeacon of Colchester; as collectors in the city and archdeaconry of London the rectors of St Bride Fleet and St Dunstan in the West Fleet Street; and as collectors in the archdeaconries of Essex, Middlesex and Colchester the abbot of Stratford Langthorne (Stratteford), the prior of Dunmow (Dunmowe) and the prior of Royston (Roystone). London 10 April 1380. [E179/67/15]

629. Mandate to William bishop of Winchester to execute the order of Simon archbishop of Canterbury, dated 12 April 1380, to make prayers and processions on solemn and festal days, Wednesdays and Fridays, with a grant of forty days' indulgence to those present, on behalf of an expedition going abroad for the good and defence of the realm. London 21 April 1380. [Reg. Wykeham ii f. 185v]

630. Certificate of John Codeford, doctor of laws, vicar-general in the absence of William bishop of London, of execution of the commission of Henry bishop of Norwich, dated 7 March 1380, for the exchange between Robert de Hull rector of Toppesfield (Toppesfeld), London diocese, and John de Roldeston rector of Butley (Betele), Norwich diocese. Given under the seal of the officiality which was to hand. London 11 May 1380. [Bodl. Libr. MS Film 651 f. 69]

631. Certificate of execution of the commission of William bishop of Winchester, dated 31 July 1380, for the exchange between Nicholas Salesbury rector of Stanford Rivers (Stanforde Ryvers), London diocese, and mr John Wylton rector of Stratfield Saye (Stratfeld Say), Winchester diocese. London 4 August 1380. [Reg. Wykeham i ff. 107v–108]

632. Certificate of execution of the commission of John bishop of Lincoln, dated 2 August 1380, for the exchange between Richard Coggeshale vicar of Arkesden, London diocese, and Nicholas de Burray master of Tolethorpe (Tolthorp) college, Lincoln diocese. Fulham manor 10 August 1380. [L.A.O. Reg. 10 ff. 219v–220]

633. Signification that John Rauff rector of West Thurrock parish church in our diocese, excommunicated for contumacy, has remained obdurate for forty days and more. London 6 September 1380. [C85/122 no. 13]

634. Signification that the persons whose names appear on the annexed schedule [now lost], excommunicated for contumacy, have remained obdurate for forty days and more. London 6 September 1380. [*Ibid.* no. 14]

635. Certificate of mr John Codeford doctor of laws, vicar-general in spirituals during the absence of William bishop of London, of execution of the commission of William bishop of Winchester, dated 17 September 1380, for the exchange between Thomas Aument rector of Beaumont, London diocese, and Thomas Draper rector of Headley (Hedele), Winchester diocese. Given under the seal of the bishop. London 25 September 1380. [Reg. Wykeham i f.108v]

636. Quitclaim by William bishop of London, John de Cobeham kt lord of Cobham (Cobeham), William de Walworth citizen of London, and Richard Warmyngton clerk, to Richard II of all their rights or titles in the manor of Pancras, with all the lands, tenements, rents, services and other appurtenances which should fall to them and to the king after the death of Robert de Knolles kt and Constance his wife in the parishes of Islington (Iseldon), Kentish Town (Kentysshtoun') and St Giles of the Lepers. London 30 September 1380. [L.R.2/61 f. 132v]

637. Mandate to John bishop of Lincoln to execute the summons of Simon archbishop of Canterbury, dated 4 October 1380, to a meeting of the convocation of the clergy of the southern province in All Saints church Northampton on 1 December 1380. London 18 October 1380. [L.A.O. Reg. 12 ff. 212v–213]

638. Certificate of execution of the commission of William bishop of Winchester, dated 9 November 1380, for the exchange between Stephen Pope rector of Little Laver, London diocese, and Robert de Barton rector of Ovington (Ovyngton), Winchester diocese. Northampton 27 November 1380. [Reg. Wykeham i ff. 111–111v]

639. Certificate of execution of the mandate of Simon archbishop of Canterbury [dated 8 October 1380] to summon the clergy of the southern province to a meeting of convocation. Northampton 30 November 1380. [Reg. Sudbury (Cant.) ff. 72–72v]

640. Commission to William Coleyn canon of [St Paul's] cathedral, in execution of a writ of 20 December 1380 ordering collection of a tax voted in All Saints church Northampton, whose terms are 22 February and 24 June 1381, which is to be levied at two rates, 6s 8d on all ecclesiastical persons over the age of sixteen, and 1s 0d on deacons, subdeacons, acolytes, those under the age of sixteen, and the notoriously poor, with the order to appoint collectors and to certify their names to the exchequer before 2 February 1381. He is to act as collector of this tax within the cathedral and the peculiar jurisdiction of the dean and chapter. Langley (Langeley) 11 January 1381. [E135/10/14]

641. Licence to Thomas bishop of Exeter to proceed to the confirming or quashing (cassacionis) in his chapel in the suburbs of the city of London or elsewhere in the diocese, of the election of dom Thomas Cullyng' to the abbacy of Tavistock, of the order of St Benedict. London 10 February 1381. [Reg. Brantingham ii f. 64]

642. Certificate of execution of the commission of John bishop of Lincoln, dated 3 March 1381, for the exchange between John Albon rector of Laindon (Leyndon), London diocese, and Roger Gerveys rector of Eton (Eton iuxta Wyndesore), Lincoln diocese. Fulham manor 5 March 1381. [L.A.O. Reg. 10 ff. 448v–449]

643. Certificate of execution of the commission of John bishop of Lincoln, dated 20 February 1381, for the exchange between John Wayte rector of Abberton (Adburton), London diocese, and Henry Everdon rector of Quarrington (Queryngton), Lincoln diocese. London 6 March 1381. [*Ibid.* f. 112v]

644. *Inspeximus* of an agreement between the vicar of Great Bardfield (Berdefeld Magna) parish church, on one side, and William Ponde, Walter Wolpet, Adam Bersle, Thomas Pollard, John Draper and John Elyn clerk of Bardfield Saling (Berdefeld Salyng), parishioners of Bardfield Saling chapel within the jurisdiction of Great Bardfield, on the other, that the chapel should be dedicated and free burial had there and all other things as in places dedicated by a bishop; in return the parishioners of Bardfield Saling will come in procession with oblations to Great Bardfield on Ascension day, instead of All Saints' day as formerly; they will offer oblations on the feast of the dedication of Great Bardfield church; and they will pay a third of a third, less a quarter, of its upkeep. Should the parishioners of Bardfield Saling default on their obligations to Great

Bardfield their chapel and cemetery will be placed under interdict. London 8 March 1381. [Guildhall Library MS 9531/3 (Reg. Braybrooke) f. 282v; see also *C.P.R. 1396–9*, 444–5]

645. Letter patent signifying that the bishop of London has caused to be dedicated the chapel of SS Peter and Paul, Bardfield Saling within the parish of Great Bardfield on 12 March 1381, and the cemetery of the same chapel on 21 March 1381, by bishop William 'Pisenensis'. London 21 March 1381. [*C.P.R. 1396–9*, 445]

646. Certificate of execution of the commission of John bishop of Lincoln, dated 25 April 1381, for the exchange between Roger Slaytbourne vicar of Hackney, London diocese, and William Fourneys rector of Quinton, Lincoln diocese. London 2 May 1381. [L.A.O. Reg. 10 f. 223v]

647. Certificate by John Codeford doctor of laws, vicar in spirituals of William bishop of London who is outside his diocese, of execution of the commission of John bishop of Lincoln, dated 1 May 1381, for the exchange between Hugh Sourdenalle chaplain of the perpetual chantry for the soul of Nicholas Crane late citizen and butcher of London in St Nicholas Shambles church, and John de Bereford vicar of Marston St Lawrence (Merssheton Laurence), Lincoln diocese. 'Given under the bishop's seal which is to hand' 18 May 1381 [*Ibid.* ff. 223v–224]

648. Certificate of Adam Mottrum vicar-general of William bishop of London who is absent, of execution of the commission of John bishop of Lincoln, dated 31 May 1381, for the exchange between John Neuton rector of Loughton (Lughton), London diocese, and William Salmont of Birdbrook rector of Welwyn, Lincoln diocese. 7 June 1381, 'sealed with the seal of William bishop of London which is to hand'. [*Ibid.* ff. 330–330v]

649. Commission to John bishop of Lincoln to effect the exchange between William Danvers rector of Horsepath (Horspathe), Lincoln diocese, and John Duffeld rector of Fryerning (Yenghospitale), London diocese. London 18 August 1381. [*Ibid.* ff. 375–375v]

650. Mandate to William bishop of Winchester to publish in all the churches of his diocese the sentence of excommunication, dated 1 September 1381, pronounced by John prior of Christ Church Canterbury against those who killed Simon late archbishop of Canterbury, sons of damnation who violently entered the palace and other manors of the archbishop against his wish and the wishes of his ministers, drank his wine and seized his goods; they broke into his prison at Maidstone (Maidenston), seized the prisoners and compelled them to depart; broke into his chase known as 'le Bruyl' in Chichester diocese and the adjacent parks; hunted, killed and took away the wild beasts there; not content with this they entered the Tower of London, beat and wounded the archbishop and finally took him outside the Tower and decapitated him, and carried his head, to which his episcopal hat was affixed by a nail in the brain, through the city shouting,

'Here is the predator's head'; then they placed it on London bridge. For all this these persons have manifestly incurred the sentence of greater excommunication. London 16 September 1381. [Reg. Wykeham ii ff. 189–189v]

651. Commission to Thomas bishop of Exeter to effect the exchange between Hugh Thornham parochial vicar of Fowey, Exeter diocese, and John Stephyn vicar of Broxbourne (Brokesbourne), London diocese. London 3 October 1381. [Reg. Brantingham ii f. 68v]

652. Signification that the persons whose names appear on the annexed schedule, excommunicated [no reason given], have remained obdurate for forty days and more. Hospice of the bishop of Worcester outside Temple Bar, London, 19 October 1381.
John vicar of Mountnessing (Gyngmounteney), John Bekyngham vicar of Writtle (Writel), Walter prior of Bedeman's Berg (Berwes), Robert rector of Creeksea (Crixhethe), Peter rector of North Shoebury (Parva Shobury), Peter rector of Great Stambridge (Magna Stanbregg), Thomas rector of Doddinghurst (Dodynghurst), William rector of Longdon Hills (Langedon), John rector of Leyton (Lutton), John vicar of Walthamstow (Welcomstowe), Robert rector of Abbess Roding (Rothyng Abbass), Hugh rector of Chipping Ongar (Aungre ad Castrum), Henry rector of Stapleford Tawney (Stapilford Tany). [C85/122 no. 15]

INDEX

References in Arabic numerals are to entry numbers and not pages.

Abberton (Essex), 643
Abel
  John, 405
  Richard, 424
Abraham (Habraham)
  John, 123; chaplain, 6
  William, 135, 144; chaplain, 111
Abyngton, William, chaplain, 107
Acta, episcopal, ix, xvii–xxiii, 547–652
Acton (Middx.), 158, 354
Acton
  John, 118
  William, 436
Administration, diocesan, xx
Aghton
  John, clerk, 16
  Nicholas, 427
Albon
  Cecily, sister, 7
  John, 126, 132, 142, 145; notary, 44;
    rector, 642
  Thomas, 436
Albotesle, Robert, 142
Aldbury (Herts.), 231
Alderker (Ellerker), Robert de, rector, 104
Aldersgate ward: within, 474–6; without,
  477–9
Aldewych, Roger, chaplain, 18
Aldgate ward, 449–52
Aldrystone, Ralph, chaplain, 104
Aleyn, William, 122; chaplain, 57
Algere, William, chaplain, 191
All Hallows Barking, chantry in, 587;
  church, 91, 117, 506
All Hallows Bread Street, church 208, 216,
  489, 491–3; parish 491–3; rector, 474
All Hallows the Great, church, 93, 538;
  parish, 538
All Hallows Honey Lane, church, 92, 543
All Hallows the Less, church, 94, 537–8
All Hallows Lombard Street, church, 155,
  203, 213, 216, 453
All Hallows London Wall, church 99;
  parish, 403; rector, 401, 596
All Hallows Staining, church, 95, 507
Ally, Thomas, 504
Alman, Bartholomew, 136
Alphamstone (Essex), 270
Alred, Richard, 194

Alswick (Herts.), 225
Altecr', John, chaplain, 111
Alvyrton, Thomas, canon, 4
Amery (Amory, Ammory, Aumory)
  Gilbert, chaplain, 178
  William, 120; chaplain, 75; rector, 602
Ampney Crucis (Gloucs.), 557
Amwell (Herts.), 245
Amy, John, rector, 601
Amys, John, chaplain, 145
Andrew
  James, 94
  John, chaplain, 35; clerk, 69
  Margaret, nun, 5
Ankerwyke (Bucks.), prioress, 409, 412
Anne, John, 134
Anstey (Herts.), 226
Ansty, John, rector, 316
Antoyne, John, 131
Appelby, John, 140, 146
Appeweyn, John, chaplain, 95
Appilton, John, 479
Aquitayne, John, chaplain of, 77
Archdeaconries: Bedford, 159; Bucking-
  ham, 159; Canterbury, 165; Chiches-
  ter, 166; Essex, 156; Hertford, 157;
  Huntingdon, 159; Leicester, 159;
  Lincoln, xi; London, xi, 628; Middle-
  sex, xii, 158, 160, 217–395, 628;
  Norfolk, 163; Northampton, 159;
  Norwich, 163; Oxford, 159; Stow, xi;
  Sudbury, 163; Worcester, 164
Archdeacons: Colchester, 140, 146, 397;
  Essex, 140; Huntingdon, 159; London,
  140, 146; Middlesex, 146
Archer (Archier)
  Elias, 211; chaplain, 76
  John, 216
  Ralph, chaplain, 39
Arderne, Richard, 510
Arkesden (Essex), 632
Arnold (Arnald)
  John, 122
  Richard, 507
Arundel
  Elizabeth, nun, 6, 197
  Thomas, bishop of Ely, xxiii, 554, 576,
    595
Aschhirst, Thomas, 469

Bate, William, 119
Bateman (Batman)
 Thomas, 135, 145
 William, bishop of Norwich, xviii n. 37
Bath and Wells, diocese, 168
Bathe, William, 132
Batman, *see* Bateman
Battersea (Surrey), 596
Baud (Baude, Bawde), John, canon, 16; rector, 88, 191
'Baudesrente', tenement called, 476
Baudry, John, chaplain, 45
Baudy, Perot, 468
Bawde, *see* Baud
Baye, William, chaplain, 96
Beaconsfield (Bekenesfeld, Bekynsfeld), Thomas (de), 122; chaplain, 9
Beauchamp (Bewchamp)
 Roger de, rector, 556
 Walter, 510
Beaumont (Essex), 605, 635
Bedeforde, John, clerk, 72
Bedeman's Berg (Essex), 652
Bedewyn (Bedewynd, Bedewynde)
 Richard, 405, 425
 Thomas, clerk, 584, 589
Bedfont (Middx.), 359, 591
Bedford, archdeaconry, 159
Bedyng, John, 502
Beeleigh (Essex), abbot, 451
Bekenesfeld, *see* Beaconsfield
Bekyngham, John, vicar, 652
Belchamp Otton (Essex), 258, 599
Belchamp St Paul's (Essex), 140, 151
Belchamp Walter (Essex), 257
Belde, William, chaplain, 69
Belgrave, William, chaplain, 43
Belgyan, William, 125
Belhomme (Belham), William, 403, 541
Bellwood (Bellewode, Belwod), John, 131; chaplain, 31
Bemoy, Richard, 468
Benedictine order, 641
Benefices, xiv; exchanges of, xvii, 548–651 *passim*
Beneger, Henry, notary, 115
Benfeld, Simon, 537
Bennett (Benet, Beneyt)
 John, 119, 135; canon, 3; chaplain, 45, 107
 Stephen, 135; chaplain, 83, 186
 Thomas, 438
Bennington, William, rector, 89
Bentley, Great (Essex), 567, 613
Bentyngford, John, canon, 3
Berden, Adam, rector, 69
Bere
 Robert (de), 155, 165; rector, 203
 Thomas, 131

Thomas de, rector, 205
Bereford (Berford), *see* Burford
Bereham, John, 472
Berkhamsted (Bercamstede, Berchamstede)
 John, clerk, 16
 William, vicar, 16
Berkyng, John, 148
Bermondsey (Surrey), 424, 446, 470, 486, 502–4, 510, 513, 531; prior, 405, 409, 418–19, 425–6, 429–30, 432, 447–8, 451, 463, 489, 494–5, 498, 532
Bermyngton, William, chaplain, 40
Bernard, Thomas, 467
Bernham, *see* Burnham
Bersaire, John, 452
Bersle, Adam, 644
Bertlot, Thomas, chaplain, 82
Bery, John, 445
Beswick (Besewyk)
 John, 126; chaplain, 182
 Robert, chaplain, 182
 Thomas, 127; chaplain, 97
Betewyk, John, chaplain, 79
Bethersden (Kent), 577
Bethlehem hospital, 11, 198, 456, 458; precinct, 459; *see also* St Mary, hospital
Betrych, Gilbert, chaplain, 75
Bette, William, celebrant, 300
Bever, Henry, 150; rector, 100, 154
Beverage (Beverache), William, rector, vicar, 308, 623
Beverley (Beverle, Bevorle, Bevyrley)
 John, 120
 John de, chaplain, 74, 110
 William, 115; canon, 393
Bewchamp, *see* Beauchamp
Bewer, Katherine, sister, 15
Biddlesden (Bucks.), abbot, 495
Biggin (Herts.), hospital, 222
Bikeliswade, Jordan, monk, 195
Billingsgate ward, 418–23
Billyngford, James de, 539
Bilney, John, 583
Birch, Little (Essex), 603
Birdbrook (Essex), 282, 648
Bisham (Berks.), prior, 436
Bishopsgate hospital, *see* St Mary Bishopsgate
Bishopsgate ward, 453–9
Bisshoppeston, John de, rector, 550
Blackburn (Blakbourne, Blakburne), William, 128; chaplain, 81
Blakdene, Alice, sister, 15
Blake, Joan, sister, 15
Blakeneye, John, 496
Blakesale, Thomas, chaplain, 11
Blakestok, Thomas, 490

Fairford (Fayrford)
Robert, vicar, 16
Walter, rector, 51; vicar, 16
Fairhode, John, 413
Faith (Feithe, Feyth), John, 136, 144
Fakenham (Fakenam)
Edmund, 520
John, 121; chaplain, 214
Fallardeston, Nicholas, chaplain, 211
Falstolf, *see* Fastolf
Fannere (Vanner, Vannere)
Agnes, 544
Henry, 481, 537
Joan, 503
Fannewright, John, 560
Faringho, John, 390
Farringdon (Faringdon, Farndon, Faryn-
don)
Roger (de), rector, 75, 178
William, 456
Farringdon ward: within, 460–5; without,
411–23
Fastolf (Falstolf), Hugh, 444, 503
Faucons, prebend, 16
Faversham (Kent), 473; abbot, 412
Fawn, John, notary, 42
Fécamp (France), abbot, 435
Feithe, *see* Faith
Felaw (Felawe), Thomas, 120, 544;
chaplain, 38
Felde, Richard, rector, 59
Felet, John, chaplain, 600
Felstead (Essex), 301
Feltham (Middx.), 360
Feltwell, Roger, 143
Ferers, Elizabeth, sister, 15
Feriby, Simon, 467
Fermour, Walter, 485
Ferrynig, Thomas, chaplain, 58
Ferthyng, Thomas, 124
Fey, John, chaplain, 5
Feyth, *see* Faith
Fille (Fylle), Robert, 130; vicar, 16
Finchingfield (Essex), 279
Finchley (Middx.), 369
Finsbury, prebend of St Paul, 521–2
Fisher (Fisshere, Fyschere), John, 136;
chaplain, 5
Fishmonger, *see* Trades
Fitzrauf, John, 563
Fitz Simon (Fysimond, Fysymond)
Ed', 482
John, 468, 506
Fitz Walter, ——, 442
Fladbury, Nicholas de, rector, 265
Flanders, 554
Flecher, Stephen, 544
Fledborough (Fledborowgh, Fleteburgh),
Peter de, 123; chaplain, 102

Flete, John, canon, 2
Fleurdelys, [sign of] the, 408
Flore, Richard, 134
Ford (Forda, Forde)
Henry, 129; chaplain, 52
John, brother, 13, 195
Forester, *see* Forster
Forneux, *see* Furness
Fornham, Nicholas, vicar, 564
Forst, Walter, vicar, 16
Forster (Forester)
John, 491; chaplain, 82
Richard, 442, 514, 522
William, 127
Foucher, William, 490
Foulham, *see* Fulham
Foulness (Essex), 626
Foun, John, 118
Fourbour
Geoffrey, 39
William, 39
Fourneys, *see* Furness
Fowey (Cornwall), 651
Foxearth (Essex), 261
Foxton, Margaret, 436
Frammelyngham, William, 510
Franc', Peter de, chaplain, 117
Francis (Franceis, Franceys, Fraunceys)
Adam, 441, 446, 455, 490, 505, 510,
531–2, 534
Agnes, 144
Elias, 442
Herbert, 132
John, rector, 180
Richard, 475
Robert, 150, 164
Frank
Henry, 534
Richard, 432
Fraternities, 397, 428, 493, 523–4, 526–7;
chaplains of, 8, 45, 119, 135
Fraunceys, *see* Francis
Fraunkeleyn, John, 434; clerk, 110
Freek, Thomas, 436
French (Frensch, Frensshe)
Cecily, nun, 5
John, 476, 489
Frend
John, chaplain, 203
Richard, 135; chaplain, 83
Freshford (Fresshford, Fressleford),
Robert, 129; chaplain, 35
Friars, *see* Austin friars, Carmelite friars,
Crutched friars
Friars minor, 520
Friars preachers, 399, 436, 465
Frowyk, Henry, 490
Fryerning (Essex), 614, 649
Fryseby, Roger, rector, 55

LONDON RECORD SOCIETY

The London Record Society was founded in December 1964 to publish transcripts, abstracts and lists of the primary sources for the history of London, and generally to stimulate interest in archives relating to London. Membership is open to any individual or institution; the annual subscription is £5 ($12) for individuals and £6 ($14) for institutions, which entitles a member to receive one copy of each volume published during the year and to attend and vote at meetings of the Society. Prospective members should apply to the Hon. Secretary, Mr Brian Burch, c/o Leicester University Library, University Road, Leicester.

The following volumes have already been published:

1. *London Possessory Assizes: a calendar*, edited by Helena M. Chew (1965)
2. *London Inhabitants within the Walls, 1695*, with an introduction by D. V. Glass (1966)
3. *London Consistory Court Wills, 1492–1547*, edited by Ida Darlington (1967)
4. *Scriveners' Company Common Paper, 1357–1628, with a continuation to 1678*, edited by Francis W. Steer (1968)
5. *London Radicalism, 1830–1843: a selection from the papers of Francis Place*, edited by D. J. Rowe (1970)
6. *The London Eyre of 1244*, edited by Helena M. Chew and Martin Weinbaum (1970)
7. *The Cartulary of Holy Trinity Aldgate*, edited by Gerald A. J. Hodgett (1971)
8. *The Port and Trade of Early Elizabethan London: documents*, edited by Brian Dietz (1972)
9. *The Spanish Company*, by Pauline Croft (1973)
10. *London Assize of Nuisance, 1301–1431: a calendar*, edited by Helena M. Chew and William Kellaway (1973)
11. *Two Calvinistic Methodist Chapels, 1743–1811: the London Tabernacle and Spa Fields Chapel*, edited by Edwin Welch (1975)
12. *The London Eyre of 1276*, edited by Martin Weinbaum (1976)
13. *The Church in London, 1375–1392*, edited by A. K. McHardy (1977)

All volumes are still in print; apply to Hon. Secretary.

The following Occasional Publication is also available:
London and Middlesex Published Records, compiled by J. M. Sims (1970)